Aspen Health Law Center Current Issues

HEALTH CARE ANTITRUST

Aspen Health Law Center Current Issues

Managed Care: State Regulation

Health Care Fraud and Abuse

Physicians as Employees

Employment Discrimination in
the Health Care Industry

Employee Benefits:
A Guide for Health Care Professionals

Health Care Antitrust

Aspen Health Law Center Current Issues

HEALTH CARE ANTITRUST

Aspen Health Law Center

AN ASPEN PUBLICATION®
Aspen Publishers, Inc.
Gaithersburg, Maryland
1998

Library of Congress Cataloging-in-Publication Data

Health care antitrust / Aspen Health Law Center.
p. cm. — (Aspen Health Law Center current issues)
Includes bibliographical references and index.
ISBN 0-8342-1227-7
1. Medical care—Law and legislation—United States.
2. Antitrust law—United States.
I. Aspen Health Law Center. II. Series.
KF3825.H415 1998
344.73'0321—dc21
98-36285
CIP

Orders: (800) 638-8437
Customer Service: (800) 234-1660

About Aspen Publishers • For more than 35 years, Aspen has been a leading professional publisher in a variety of disciplines. Aspen's vast information resources are available in both print and electronic formats. We are committed to providing the highest quality information available in the most appropriate format for our customers. Visit Aspen's Internet site for more information resources, directories, articles, and a searchable version of Aspen's full catalog, including the most recent publications: **http://www.aspenpublishers.com**

Aspen Publishers, Inc. • The hallmark of quality in publishing
Member of the worldwide Wolters Kluwer group.

Editorial Services: Jane Colilla
Library of Congress Catalog Card Number: 98-36285
ISBN: 0-8342-1227-7

Printed in the United States of America

1 2 3 4 5

Table of Contents

Preface

This book, *Health Care Antitrust,* is part of a collection of reference products addressing issues of current interest in the field of health care law. These products are designed to provide up-to-date, easy-to-retrieve information on a variety of topics selected on the basis of their relevance to late-breaking developments in the health care industry. The subjects covered in the inaugural group of products include *Managed Care: State Regulation, Physicians as Employees, Employment Discrimination in the Health Care Industry, Employee Benefits: A Guide for Health Care Professionals,* and *Health Care Fraud and Abuse.* Other topics will be added to this legal reference series as the need arises.

The books are designed to provide practical overviews of the principal legal issues relating to each topic. They are extensively footnoted, and a Table of Contents and Index provide easy access to the information. Most of the products also offer a selection of support documents, including statutory text, model contract language, and administrative rulings and guidance.

The series is compiled by the attorneys and editors on staff at the Health Law and Compliance Center of Aspen Publishers, who contributed to developing these products through their writing and research efforts. We hope that these products, either separately or as a group, will meet the busy health care professional's ongoing need for information in the rapidly evolving field of health care law.

INTRODUCTION

Antitrust laws touch upon a wide range of conduct and business relationships in the delivery of health care services, and the issues that should be of concern to health care organizations (i.e., hospitals, HMOs, and other managed care organizations) are described in this current issues book. The objective of this book is to provide a general understanding of antitrust analysis as applied to contractual relationships and business strategies that present antitrust risks in a managed care environment.

Although increased comprehension of federal antitrust law and related issues may decrease a health care organization's exposure to risk, it is important to remember that antitrust laws have been developed by the courts, and as a result, the analysis of antitrust risks is fact intensive. The courts apply general antitrust principles to a particular market setting; thus, risk managers and health care administrators should recognize that a determination of antitrust liability will be evaluated on the merits of each case, and that differences in market and in structuring arrangements may result in different judicial or administrative outcomes.

Beyond the case law, health care professionals assessing antitrust risks may turn to guidance from the federal antitrust enforcement agencies—the Department of Justice (DOJ) and the Federal Trade Commission (FTC)—and in particular, to the agencies' revised *Statements of Antitrust Enforcement Policy in Health Care* (hereinafter *1996 Policy Statements*). These guidelines, as well as case law of particular significance to the mergers and a variety of other conduct and contractual relationships that have been used to provide managed care, are covered extensively in this book.

OVERVIEW: FEDERAL ANTITRUST STATUTES

There are three principal federal antitrust statutes applicable to the health care industry: the Sherman Act,[1] the Clayton Act,[2] and the Federal Trade Commission Act.[3] Also relevant, but not discussed extensively in this book, are amendments to the Clayton Act: the Robinson-Patman Act,[4] which prohibits certain practices that result in discriminatory pricing,[5] and the Celler-Kefauver Act,[6] relating to the Clayton Act's provisions concerning corporate mergers. These basic antitrust statutes are discussed in more detail in the following sections.[7]

The Sherman Act

The Sherman Act of 1890 was intended to provide a more significant deterrent than common law prohibitions on anticompetitive activities by establishing civil and criminal sanctions applicable to participants in anticompetitive arrangements. Under the Sherman Act, the government was granted the authority to initiate criminal prosecution against parties to restrictive agreements and monopolies. In addition, the government was granted the power to seek injunctive relief.

After much debate and several drafts, the legislation ultimately defined antitrust violations in broad, general terms, basically prohibiting concerted actions that constitute unreasonable restraints of trade. Section 1 of the Sherman Act provides:

> [E]very contract, combination in the form of trust or otherwise, or conspiracy, in restraint of trade or commerce among the several States, or with foreign nations, is hereby declared to be illegal.[8]

Also prohibited, under Section 2 of the Act, are monopolization and attempted monopolization; that section provides:

> Every person who shall monopolize, or attempt to monopolize, or combine or conspire with any other person or persons, to monopolize any part of the trade or commerce among the several States, or with foreign nations, shall be deemed guilty of a felony.[9]

The Clayton Act

By 1914, Congress had determined that additional legislation was required to complement the broad prohibitions of the Sherman Act. With the enactment of the Clayton Act, certain specific practices of single entities—price discrimination,[10] exclusive dealing and tying arrangements,[11] and mergers[12]—

that would tend to lessen competition or create a monopoly were declared illegal. Significantly, under the Sherman Act, an activity must have an actual adverse effect on competition before it is considered illegal; however, under the Clayton Act, an activity that might substantially lessen competition may be illegal. The Clayton Act therefore addresses practices in their incipience that, if carried to their logical conclusion, would lead to a monopoly.

Perhaps most important, Congress authorized in the Clayton Act private antitrust enforcement and a treble damages remedy.[13] By granting injured persons the right to sue and recover significant damages if successful, Congress provided a powerful financial incentive to refrain from anticompetitive behavior.

The Federal Trade Commission Act

Also in 1914, Congress enacted the Federal Trade Commission (FTC) Act,[14] which declared "unfair methods of competition" to be illegal. More specifically, Section 5 of the Act provides:

> Unfair methods of competition in or affecting commerce, and unfair or deceptive acts or practices in or affecting commerce, are hereby declared unlawful.[15]

This broad proscription was intended to ensure that antitrust enforcement would not be limited to the specific activities prohibited by the Clayton Act. Not surprisingly, the FTC Act has been interpreted as broader than the Sherman and Clayton Acts, and most Sherman Act violations are also violations of the FTC Act. The government antitrust enforcement agency, the FTC, was created by the FTC Act, which authorized the agency to enforce the substantive provisions of both the FTC and Clayton Acts.

Application of Antitrust Statutes to Health Care

For a long time, the health care industry was widely believed to be exempt from the antitrust laws. The activities of individual health care providers, such as physicians, were considered outside the scope of the antitrust laws, because they involved "learned professions," as distinguished from trade or business. Over the years, the scope of this "exemption" was limited, and its validity was often challenged.[16] These challenges reflected a growing public perception that the activities of those in learned professions were not entirely different from the activities of those in trade or business and that some such activities were anticompetitive in purpose and effect.

It was not until 1975, however, that the U.S. Supreme Court, in *Goldfarb v. Virginia State Bar*,[17] abolished any remnants of a blanket exemption from the federal antitrust laws for the learned professions. Although *Goldfarb* involved the activities of lawyers, its reasoning has been applied to other professions, including health care.[18] Although there are limitations to the applicability of antitrust laws, the health care organization today is particularly susceptible to circumstances that may give rise to antitrust liability; for example, to pinpoint a few of these circumstances, the health care organization must pay close attention to potential for antitrust risk whenever it:

- Has a significant market share
- Takes action jointly with other health care organizations, physicians, or third-party payers
- Denies privileges to any professional or limits privileges of a professional on the staff (including denials of privileges related to exclusive agreements)[19]
- Is involved in an acquisition, merger, joint venture, provider network, or other integrated delivery system

Following three additional background sections covering antitrust enforcement, fundamental antitrust principles, and exemptions (discussed next in that order), some of the antitrust issues related to these activities will be discussed in greater detail.

ANTITRUST ENFORCEMENT

To evaluate an entity's degree of antitrust exposure accurately, it is necessary to consider whether the potential plaintiffs are likely to bring a lawsuit challenging conduct or transactions harmful to competition. The potential plaintiffs that must be considered include the Antitrust Division of the DOJ, the FTC, state attorneys general, and individuals harmed by anticompetitive actions. In a sense, each of these categories, discussed in greater detail in the following sections, represents potential enforcers of the antitrust statutes.

Department of Justice

The Antitrust Division of the DOJ has primary responsibility for enforcing federal antitrust laws. This responsibility includes investigation of possible violations of both the criminal and civil provisions of the Sherman, Clayton, and Robinson-Patman Acts. The DOJ investigates possible criminal violations of antitrust laws by initiating a proceeding before a grand jury. The grand jury has broad investigative powers; it may compel witnesses to testify and may require the presentation of books, documents, records, and other information. Unlike trial juries, which determine guilt or innocence, a grand jury merely determines whether a party charged with violating an antitrust law should stand trial. If, after the examination of witnesses, documents, and other presented evidence, the grand jury finds probable cause to believe that a criminal antitrust violation has occurred, it returns an indictment setting forth the practice alleged to be in violation of the law.

If the indictment results in a conviction under the Sherman Act, a corporation may be fined a maximum of $10 million. Individuals, partnerships, and unincorporated associates are subject to imprisonment not exceeding three years and/or a maximum fine of $350,000.[20] The penalties that may be imposed under the Clayton Act are considerably smaller; the maximum fine provided under that Act is $5,000 and the maximum length of imprisonment is one year.[21]

The DOJ also may initiate civil investigations pursuant to the Civil Process Act[22] to determine whether a party has violated any civil provision of the antitrust laws. If the civil investigation indicates that a violation has occurred, the DOJ may institute a civil suit, seeking an injunction or damages. Although the DOJ may recover only actual damages in bringing a civil enforcement action, a defendant that loses in a government enforcement suit also faces the possibility that a private plaintiff will employ the decision in a subsequent treble damage action.

Because of this additional exposure, a defendant may wish to enter into a consent decree under the Antitrust Procedures and Penalties Act.[23] In essence, consent decrees are negotiated settlements entered before any testimony is taken. These decrees not only save both parties substantial time and expense, but also provide a wide range of enforcement remedies, including divestiture or dissolution. Although consent decrees are made without admissions by any party, once the court enters the final order, these decrees have the same force and effect as decrees entered in litigated cases, except that they do not constitute prima facie evidence in any subsequent private treble damages action.

The DOJ monitors compliance with antitrust judgments by means of the civil investigative process. Through this process, the DOJ can compel a health care organization against which an antitrust judgment has been entered to produce records that indicate whether the organization is in compliance with the judgment. Noncompliance can result in the initiation of contempt proceedings.[24]

Federal Trade Commission

The FTC, empowered by the FTC Act to investigate and order the cessation of unfair methods of competition, enforces the substantive provisions of the FTC Act but also, in cooperation with the DOJ, enforces Clayton Act provisions that prohibit price discrimination, exclusive dealings and similar arrangements, certain corporate acquisitions of stock or assets, and interlocking directorates. To facilitate their cooperative efforts, the DOJ and the FTC issued written procedures in 1993, which refine the agencies' system for dividing antitrust enforcement responsibilities.[25] The main element in deciding which agency will pursue an investigation that falls within the jurisdiction of both agencies is which agency has gained the most expertise in the product involved.

The FTC may investigate an alleged antitrust violation on its own initiative or at the request of the President, Congress, another government agency, the U.S. Attorney General, courts, or other persons.[26] The broad investigative authority extends throughout FTC activities, from investigations of alleged violations of antitrust laws to investigations of compliance with antitrust decrees issued under the Clayton or FTC Acts.[27] The investigative function is effectuated mainly through subpoenas and civil investigative demands. Prior to an adjudication of the case's merits, an FTC investigation may be terminated by entry of a consent order. Like consent decrees, consent orders that are entered prior to adjudicative proceedings have the same force and effect as a court order.

The FTC also is authorized to institute civil penalty actions against those who knowingly violate the FTC Act and to petition a court for a temporary restraining order or a preliminary injunction in appropriate circumstances.[28] Courts have generally interpreted this power as authorization for the FTC to seek any equitable remedy judicially appropriate; the FTC does not, however, have the power to seek damages for antitrust violations.

State Attorneys General

Both state and federal antitrust laws are enforced by state attorneys general,[29] and state officials responsible for antitrust enforcement usually have available an array of enforcement procedures comparable to those of the federal agencies. For example, state grand juries often have wide latitude in criminal investigations and may investigate activities outside the state if the impact of the alleged criminal conduct has been felt in the state. In many states, the scope of the state civil investigative demand procedures is comparable to that of the DOJ and the FTC. The states' subpoena and investigative powers are also similar to federal procedures and extend to all information relevant to the investigation.

State enforcement agencies have also utilized consent decrees to impose a wide range of remedies, including fines, penalties, and attorneys' fees or investigative fees payable to the state. In general, the types of penalties imposed by state antitrust law parallel those imposed by federal antitrust law, but they vary in severity from state to state.[30] Several states impose only fines and/or imprisonment as the penalties for antitrust violations. The majority of states, however, provide for injunctive relief, ouster of out-of-state corporations, or the forfeiture of corporate charters or property, as well as fines and/or imprisonment.[31]

The DOJ and the FTC have adopted a joint protocol for cooperating with the states in merger investigations.[32] If a state agency is involved in the review or investigation of the transaction, the merging entities should be prepared to deal with the state agency's concerns.[33] As will be discussed in a later section of this book, the attorney general in some states may be more likely to enter into a regulatory decree to resolve its concerns; a merging entity should carefully consider, however, the consequences of entering into such a decree and the extent to which it will be able to comply with the decree's terms. [For a more detailed discussion, see Mergers and Acquisitions among Private Hospitals, under State Action Immunity.]

Private Enforcement

Section 4 of the Clayton Act authorizes treble damage awards to "any person who shall be injured in his business or property by reason of anything forbidden in the antitrust laws."[34] In addition, Section 16 of that Act entitles a private party to sue for injunctive relief against threatened loss or damage by a violation of the antitrust laws.[35] To successfully assert an antitrust claim, however, a private plaintiff is required to demonstrate three standing requirements: (1) a violation of the antitrust laws; (2) injury to its business or property or in the case of injunction, threatened loss or damage; and (3) a causal relationship between the antitrust violation and the injury.

Probably the most important of these three requirements is injury to business or property (i.e., injury to commercial interests or enterprises). In actions for treble damages, private plaintiffs' access to the courts is limited when they are injured only indirectly by the antitrust activity.[36] When the injury is direct, however, courts have held that private plaintiffs have standing under the antitrust laws in a variety of different situations involving diverse injuries, including those that: cause increases in the cost of doing business; cause loss of business, including good will and reputation; and frustrate a serious potential competitor's attempts to enter the market.[37]

In actions seeking injunctive relief, proof of threatened injury or loss may be sufficient to constitute injury to business or property. Actual injury need not be shown; rather, to obtain relief, a private plaintiff need demonstrate only a significant threat of injury from an impending, continuing, or recurring antitrust violation. In the case of a merger, a private party can sue for injunctive relief against the transaction even if the DOJ and the FTC have approved the merger. A state or a private litigant may still have grounds for pursuing a private right of action, and in doing so, may challenge and potentially prevent a merger or seek divestiture of a completed merger.[38]

FUNDAMENTAL ANTITRUST PRINCIPLES

The antitrust principles outlined in this section address three central aspects of antitrust law:

1. Requirements of an antitrust claim under the Sherman Act
2. The type of antitrust analysis to be applied to the alleged anticompetitive conduct (e.g., the rule of reason versus per se rule), and
3. Assuming rule-of-reason treatment, how does the alleged anticompetitive conduct impact upon the market of products or services in which the conduct takes place? (e.g., how is market power assessed and does such power amount to monopolization?)

Although additional concepts are important to the analysis of particular transactions (e.g., mergers and acquisitions, joint ventures, etc.), an understanding of these fundamental concepts is essential to undertaking a knowledgeable antitrust review of any conduct or transaction that may adversely affect competition.

Interstate Commerce Requirement

The federal antitrust laws apply, by their own terms, only to activities that are in commerce or that have an effect on commerce. Thus, activities that are purely local in nature and effect fall outside the scope of the federal antitrust laws, although state laws may be applicable. In applying the "effects on interstate commerce test," the federal appeals courts are divided. Some invoke the Sherman Act when any business activity of the defendant affects interstate commerce; other courts invoke it when the particular business activity challenged affects interstate commerce.[39] In *Summit Health, Ltd. v. Pinhas,*[40] the Supreme Court ruled that a physician was not required to prove an actual effect on interstate commerce to support federal jurisdiction.

As a practical matter, the business activities of virtually all health care organizations have an effect on interstate commerce: patients travel interstate, insurance payments are received from interstate sources, supplies are purchased from interstate vendors, and physicians are recruited in interstate efforts. Thus, although some lower courts have dismissed federal cases based on the failure to allege or prove interstate commerce, many such decisions have been overturned on appeal, and the overwhelming majority of courts have recognized interstate commerce in health care antitrust cases.[41]

Standards of Legality

A literal interpretation of the Sherman Act would result in the prohibition of virtually all contracts, as every contract restrains trade in one way or another. Merely purchasing syringes from one vendor, for example, effectively precludes another vendor from supplying syringes to the same hospital at that time. The courts, however, have recognized that Congress intended to prohibit only unreasonable restraints of trade, and in applying antitrust laws have developed a basic analytical framework that relies upon two central standards of legality: (1) the per se rule and (2) the rule of reason.

Per Se Rule

The Supreme Court has held that, although most restraints of trade must be analyzed in terms of the nature, purpose, and effect of the restraint (in other words, under a rule-of-reason analysis as discussed in the next section), some types of restraints are so inimical to competition and so unjustified that they will be conclusively presumed to be illegal. These types of restraints are called per se violations.

The per se antitrust standard reflects the judgment that, within certain categories of restraints, cases that do not fit the general rule "are not sufficiently common or important to justify the time and expense necessary to identify them."[42] The standard is a rule of judicial economy, permitting courts to find a violation upon the simple proof of an agreement. The primary effect of the per se standard, therefore, is to dispense with the need for elaborate proof concerning the competitive and economic effects of the challenged practice. As the Supreme Court stated in *Northern Pacific Railway Co. v. United States:*

> There are certain agreements or practices which because of their pernicious effect on competition and lack of any redeeming virtue are conclusively presumed to be unreasonable and therefore illegal without elaborate inquiry as to the precise harm they have caused or the business excuse for their use.[43]

The Court went on to explain that horizontal agreements between competitors that constitute price fixing, market allocation, or group boycott, and certain tying arrangements are among the practices that have been widely recognized by the courts to be unlawful in and of themselves.

All three types of horizontal arrangements among competitors have been held to be per se illegal under the Sherman Act. Tying arrangements (vertical agreements that involve the exercise of market power by a single firm) have been held to be per se illegal under the Clayton Act when they restrain a substantial amount of commerce. All other types of arrangements that arguably restrain trade are subject to evaluation under the rule of reason, although it is not uncommon for certain per se violations to be analyzed under the rule of reason.[44]

It is also worth noting that an arrangement that would typically fall under rule-of-reason treatment may be susceptible to per se analysis. For example, some arrangements to negotiate jointly or to disseminate data among competitors may approach antitrust-sensitive issues such as price, and thereby enter the realm of a per se illegal price-fixing charge. Moreover, health care organizations should be aware that any horizontal agreement among competitors is inherently suspect and potentially subject to the per se rule.

The applicability of the per se rule to the health care industry, however, may in some cases be limited by the judicial tenet that the presumption of illegality is reserved for those classes of restraints that experience indicates "would always or almost always tend to restrict competition and decrease output."[45] In several lower federal court decisions, the per se rule has been rejected as inapplicable to health care defendants because of the lack of judicial experience necessary to characterize many health care practices as plainly anticompetitive.[46]

Certain types of restraints, however, have been found subject to the per se rule, regardless of whether or not the case involves medical professionals and their conduct in operating a health care practice. In *Arizona v. Maricopa County Medical Society,*[47] for example, the Supreme Court held that maximum fee setting by a group of physicians was subject to the per se rule of illegality. It concluded that, with respect to price-fixing agreements, the Sherman Act establishes one uniform rule applicable to all industries alike—that is, that such agreements are per se unlawful. The Court found unpersuasive an argument that the per se rule should not be applied to the case because of the judiciary's inexperience in applying antitrust laws to the health care industry. Although acknowledging that professional practices premised on public service or ethical norms may, in some contexts, warrant different treatment, the Court ultimately concluded that this exception did not apply to the physicians' horizontal price-fixing agreements.

Even after the *Maricopa* decision was rendered, however, federal courts generally have been reluctant to apply the per se standard to activities of health care providers, particularly where the providers are acting in the public interest, rather than their own commercial interest.[48]

Rule of Reason

In situations where restraints of trade other than per se violations are involved, the legal analysis follows what is commonly called the "rule of reason" approach. In *Chicago Board of Trade v. United States,* the Supreme Court set forth the rule-of-reason standard of legality as applied to alleged violations of the Sherman Act:

> The true test of legality is whether the restraint imposed is such as merely regulates and perhaps thereby promotes competition or whether it is such as may suppress or even destroy competition. To determine that question the Court must ordinarily consider the facts peculiar to the business to which the restraint is applied; its condition before and after the restraint was imposed; the nature of the restraint and its effect, actual or probable.[49]

This test can be applied to virtually every allegedly anticompetitive practice.

Analysis under the rule of reason requires that an activity be evaluated on the basis of its intent, competitive impact, and breadth, in view of the need. A court assesses the motive for the activity and weighs its procompetitive effects against any anticompetitive effects. Alternately, a court might determine whether the restraint is ancillary to a procompetitive purpose. The comprehensive nature of the rule-of-reason analysis renders it difficult to administer, and prosecution of cases under the rule of reason is expensive and time consuming. Moreover, its predictive value to guide future conduct is limited because decisions under the rule of reason depend largely on the particular facts of each case.

Under certain circumstances, courts have condemned restraints under the rule-of-reason standard without resorting to a full rule-of-reason analysis. Usually such restraints involve conduct that could fall under the per se standard (e.g., horizontal price fixing or market division), but the court has decided to refrain from applying that standard. In these cases, the depth of the court's inquiry is often less than the comprehensive market analysis that generally is required under the rule of reason. In applying this middle standard in a case involving a group of dentists who conspired to withhold X-rays requested by dental insurers for evaluating benefits claims, for example, the Supreme Court refused to invoke the per se rule under the theory that the dentists' policy constituted a group boycott.[50] In choosing instead to apply the rule of reason, the Court held that "the finding of actual, sustained adverse effects in competition in those areas where the group of dentists predominated . . . is legally sufficient to support a finding that the challenged restraint was unreasonable even in the absence of elaborate market analysis."[51]

Definition of Concerted Action

The Sherman Act prohibits "contracts, combinations and conspiracies" in restraint of trade. Many of the activities to which this applies are obvious. For example, a direct agreement between two hospitals to charge the same price for an appendectomy is certainly one kind of agreement prohibited by the antitrust laws. A joint venture falls within the provisions of both the Sherman Act and the Clayton Act. Whether certain other activities are considered prohibited concerted actions is not, however, always clear.

For the most part, concerted action refers to joint activity by competitors (i.e., horizontal agreements). Thus, although sales agreements between two parties quite literally fix the price of a commodity or service between the two parties, such agreements are beyond the intended reach of the antitrust laws.[52] Nevertheless, courts have assumed that such agreements can be described as concerted action and have considered the merits of antitrust claims in these circumstances.[53] The Supreme Court has ruled that to determine that a price-fixing conspiracy exists, there must be direct or circumstantial evidence that reasonably tends to prove a conscious commitment to a common scheme designed to achieve an unlawful objective.[54]

The antitrust implications of sales arrangements between two parties (i.e., vertical agreements) should be considered when:

- the purchaser or seller has a very large market share
- the agreement requires that one party deal exclusively with the other
- the agreement makes the purchase of the desired product or service conditional on the purchase of another product or service (i.e., a tying arrangement)
- prices charged to different competitors for identical goods or services purchased during the same time period are different (i.e., price discrimination)

Proof of Concerted Activities

The most common antitrust violations result from concerted or collusive activities by two or more competitors. Such activities resulting in a restraint on competition are prohibited by Section 1 of the Sherman Act and by the FTC Act. An important aspect of these antitrust claims is the standard for proving the existence of illegal concerted activities. A plaintiff must show not only that defendants are legally capable of conspiring, but that they actually did so.

Federal courts have consistently held that evidence of an illegal contract or conspiracy does not require any formal agreement; in many antitrust cases, unlawful agreement or conspiracy is sufficiently demonstrated by circumstantial evidence.[55] Nonetheless, physicians bringing antitrust lawsuits have experienced considerable difficulty in demonstrating the requisite meeting of minds in an unlawful arrangement. Federal courts have consistently recognized that mere contacts and communications, or the mere opportunity to conspire, are insufficient evidence from which to infer a conspiracy.[56]

Establishing Unreasonable Restraint of Trade

Once it has been determined that defendants in an antitrust case have the legal capacity to conspire and that there is a horizontal or vertical agreement, the effect of that agreement must be considered to determine whether it restrains competition unreasonably. The plaintiff seeking to establish the unreasonableness of a particular trade restraint must demonstrate from the facts an actual and unreasonable harm to competition. Ordinarily, the existence of market power is an essential ingredient to such a showing under the rule of reason.[57]

Market Power

At the very core of antitrust law is the intent to remedy abuses associated with the aggregation and maintenance of market power. Theoretically, a seller operating in a highly concentrated market is more likely to accrue monopoly profits than a seller in an unconcentrated market. Monopoly profits cause not only economic harm to consumers in the concentrated market, but also an economic disallocation of resources from other markets.

Any competitor in the market can acquire and legitimately maintain market power. Antitrust issues are raised, however, whenever a single firm employs unfair methods to acquire or maintain market power, or when two or more firms combine to aggregate their market power. Any practice that arguably could affect competition may be subject to antitrust scrutiny.

Whenever a health care organization possesses significant market power or deals with a firm or a group that has significant market power, antitrust implications should be considered. Violations of Section 2 of the Sherman Act (i.e., monopolizations and attempted monopolizations) are determined partly by market power. Under Section 7 of the Clayton Act, market power also relates directly to the legality of mergers, joint ventures, and other provider networks. Moreover, market power is an element of illegal tying and exclusive dealing arrangements prohibited by Section 3 of the Clayton Act, as well as unreasonably restrictive agreements prohibited by Section 1 of the Sherman Act.

To determine an institution's market power, it is first necessary to identify the market in which the firm may exercise power. For antitrust purposes, the relevant market has two components: (1) a product component and (2) a geographic component.

Product Market

The relevant product market involves the product or service at issue and all substantially acceptable substitutes for it. Essentially, the extent of the relevant product market is determined by the entire range of products that are reasonably interchangeable for the consumer's use.[58] In making this determination, courts have also inquired into commercial realities, such as buyer preferences, physical differences, and established trade practices.[59] In addition, consideration should be given to the probability that new competitors will enter the market as a result of price increases.

Because health care organizations provide a wide variety of services, it may be difficult to ascertain the scope of the relevant product market in any particular case. There is some question as to whether the relevant product market for the organization's services should be characterized as a single market consisting of a variety of services or as a series of markets for individual services, such as coronary, psychiatric, or maternity care.[60]

The cluster-of-services approach certainly provides a useful shorthand method for determining market power. The accuracy of this approach to assess market power share depends on particular market conditions, however. For example, when hospitals compete with nonhospital health care institutions, such as ambulatory surgicenters and birthing centers, the cluster approach would tend to overestimate a hospital's market power. Alternately, if one hospital has a particularly large coronary care facility as compared with that of other hospitals, the cluster approach would tend to underestimate its market power.

Because consumers of health care services are likely to be interested in obtaining a particular service, rather than a cluster of services,[61] viewing particular types of services as unique product markets generally results in a more accurate definition of the relevant product market. This approach, which has been followed by the majority of courts, takes into account the full range of options available to consumers. For example, courts have distinguished between the practice of dentistry and prepaid dental care;[62] between adult open-heart surgery and pediatric open-heart surgery;[63] and between inpatient psychiatric care provided by private psychiatric hospitals and nongovernment, general, acute care hospitals, and inpatient psychiatric care provided by state-owned psychiatric facilities.[64]

As hospitals continue to diversify into ancillary markets, the issue of market power will become an important one if a hospital is challenged by a competitor. In one case, for example, a hospital that acquired a smaller community hospital, and subsequently converted the smaller entity into a facility providing subacute health care services such as rehabilitation, was sued by physicians operating a competing medical clinic who alleged numerous antitrust violations.[65] Unpersuaded by the physicians' arguments that the traditional product market definition for hospital mergers and acquisitions—acute care inpatient hospital services—must apply in this case, the court concluded that dramatic technological changes within the medical field have changed market analysis in these cases. The court was swayed by the competing medical clinic's assertion that the relevant product market is both inpatient and outpatient hospital services, including at least general acute care hospitals, all types of outpatient surgery centers, birthing centers, and home health care companies. After reviewing expert opinions on the question of whether the relevant market should include nonhospital providers, the court found that many of the procedures that used to be performed only in a hospital now are performed on an outpatient basis, and thus declined to decide the appropriate parameters of the relevant product market on a motion for summary judgment.

Hospital mergers have increased dramatically in the past decade in response to managed care activities. One implication is that, with managed care, formerly defined "local markets" for antitrust purposes now may be part of regional markets for the delivery of health care services, which in turn has implications for the definition of relevant product market. In one recent case, for example, the DOJ unsuccessfully attempted to block the proposed merger of the two largest hospital networks in Long Island, New York, by convincing a federal district court in that state to accept a relevant product market more narrowly drawn than the product market historically used in hospital merger cases—that is, general acute inpatient services.[66] The merging entities in this case were two teaching hospitals, each of which is affiliated with a well-known school of medicine, that are located just two miles apart. The larger of the two hospitals has 720 acute, nonpsychiatric inpatient beds, making it the largest and most prestigious hospital in a system of nine hospitals located on Long Island and in surrounding counties, while the other hospital is an equally well-known institution with 591 acute, nonpsychiatric inpatient beds. The DOJ's complaint was based on a novel theory of anchor hospital systems, which is premised on the fact that, as portrayed by the DOJ, the two hospitals are the largest and most reputable in their service offerings, and therefore any managed care plan in the area would need to include at least one of the hospitals to "anchor" its provider network to attract customers. According to allegations in the DOJ's complaint, with both anchor hospital systems merging into one hospital system, there would be no reason for the anchor hospitals to compete for the business of managed care plans, and without such competition, health care consumers will face higher prices.

In dismissing the complaint (including the DOJ's request to permanently enjoin the merger of the two hospital systems), the court determined that the DOJ failed to prove that the merger will substantially lessen competition, and therefore failed to establish its claims under Section 7 of the Clayton Act. Among other reasons for rejecting the DOJ's claims, the court disagreed with the DOJ's definition of the relevant product market as "acute inpatient services provided by anchor hospitals to managed care plans," finding this definition to be unduly restricted to the two anchor hospitals. Emphasizing the DOJ's failure to establish that acute inpatient services provided at the anchor hospitals are unique and therefore comprise their own relevant product market, the court opted for the more traditional product market definition in hospital merger cases—"general acute inpatient services." Although conceding that such services are available at other area hospitals, the DOJ argued that the reputation of the anchor hospitals is the primary factor supporting a separate and distinct relevant product market. The court found the "reputation" factor problematic because it is based on the perception of where patients currently go, rather than where they could practically go in the future for acute care inpatient services. Moreover, the court concluded that such a narrowly drawn product market fails to factor in the dynamics of an intensely competitive urban health care market in which consumers can and do seek medical care from other Long Island non-anchor hospitals as well as from world-class hospital systems based in Manhattan. Similar reasoning underlies the court's rejection of the DOJ's proposed relevant geographic market in this case and in other hospital merger cases.[67]

Geographic Market

The relevant geographic market is "the market area in which the seller operates, and to which the purchaser can practically turn for supplies."[68] Thus, to ascertain the boundaries of the geographic market (i.e., the area of effective competition), economic and physical barriers to expansion such as transportation cost, delivery limitations, customer convenience, and customer preferences must be considered.[69]

The primary factors that courts have examined to determine the relevant geographic market for health care services include:

- patient flow statistics
- physician admitting practices
- medical staff lists at various health care organizations
- third-party payer practices
- marketing activities of physicians and health care organizations in the area
- public perception

From an economic perspective, probably the most significant factor is patient flow data, because these statistics provide a numerical result. Under one proposed criterion, the geographic area in which 75 percent of a hospital's patients reside constitutes a market for antitrust purposes if 75 percent of the residents obtain services at the hospital.[70] The court in *United States v. Rockford Memorial Corp.*[71] used this so-called Elzinga-Hogarty test as well as other factors when setting the bounds of the geographic market.

Although this test is useful to approximate the market, it is inherently limited; it describes the current state of the market, but does not take market dynamics into account. Courts increasingly are rejecting health care antitrust cases that do not take into account the dynamic of the rapidly changing market for health care services.[72]

In *Federal Trade Commission v. Freeman,*[73] for example, the FTC's narrow definition of the relevant geographic market was criticized, and ultimately rejected, for not giving adequate consideration to market dynamics. The case involved the merger of the second and third largest acute care hospitals in Joplin, Missouri. Seeking to form a new nonprofit organization, the second largest hospital, a 158-bed general acute care allopathic hospital, negotiated with the smallest of the three hospitals in the area, a financially troubled osteopathic hospital. In addition to these two hospitals, there were several other allopathic hospitals in the area. The FTC challenged the merger, but the trial court accepted the geographic market definition put forth by the hospitals, rather than that proposed by the government. While the FTC's defined service area was restricted to a 27-mile radius of Joplin (based on hospital admissions records and patient flow statistics indicating percentage of residents who obtain services at the relevant hospitals), the service area put forth by the hospitals extended much further geographically.

Emphasizing the hospitals' reliance on evidence indicating not just where patients actually go for acute inpatient care, but also where patients could turn for such services, an appeals court upheld the lower court's preference for the hospitals' product market definition, which extended the market to include 17 hospitals (12 of which were within 40 miles of Joplin and 5 of which were between 40 and 50 miles of that city). Criticizing the FTC's more limited definition based on percentages taken from hospital admissions records, the court held that the FTC's evidence was insufficient to establish a relevant geographic market. By focusing on only current competitor perceptions and current consumer habits, and giving no indication of where patients could practically turn for alternative sources, the FTC's data failed to reflect the dynamic nature of the relevant geographic health care market, the court explained.

It is also worth noting that the scope of the geographic market depends on the scope of the relevant product market. For example, patient flow statistics might change markedly if new competitors, including specialty clinics, established themselves in the area. Accordingly, evaluation of patient flow data and other factors used to determine relevant geographic market should be reviewed for inpatient and outpatient services as well as for the types of inpatient services utilized by patients who cross geographic lines (i.e., general inpatient or unique, specialized services). In *Robinson v. Magovern*,[74] for example, the size of the relevant geographic market for adult open-heart surgery was determined by the nature of the service itself. The court rejected both the plaintiff's and the defendant's defined geographic market; the plaintiff had argued that the market consisted of two counties surrounding Pittsburgh, Pennsylvania, while the defendant contended that there was a nationwide market for adult open-heart surgery. Opting for a definition between the two extremes, the federal district court relied on evidence showing that a high percentage of adults having open-heart surgeries in a 16-county area surrounding Pittsburgh had their surgeries performed at one of six hospitals in Pittsburgh; therefore, this 16-county area was the relevant geographic market area. In reaching this conclusion, the court specifically noted that the community served by a hospital expands as the service becomes more specialized.[75]

Evaluating Market Power in the Relevant Market

Once the relevant market has been defined, the next step is to determine whether the parties have market power within that market; this is often determined through calculating market share. Whether the market share is sufficiently high to expose a health care organization to antitrust liability depends on the factors in each case. Perhaps the most common approach for proving (or disproving) the existence of market power is the presentation of circumstantial evidence of market share and barriers to entry. For purposes of determining whether antitrust implications should be scrutinized, a threshold of approximately 30 percent appears to be a good rule of thumb in most cases.

Market share alone is not enough to evaluate market power, however. Although market share evidence is important and may give rise to presumptions, it is not conclusive proof of the existence or absence of market power.[76] The analysis of entry barriers also is significant because high barriers to entry into the market mean greater market power for the dominant market participants. On the contrary, market power is lessened by the entry of new service providers into the market; without barriers to entry, even a firm with a high market share could not profitably raise prices because it would lose its market share as others charging a competitive price entered the market.[77] Thus, characteristics of the relevant market directly impact upon the evaluation of market power, and particularly upon the determination of whether a high percentage of market share demonstrates market power.

Monopolies

The evils commonly associated with restrictive agreements held illegal under Section 1 of the Sherman Act are potentially even greater when a market becomes monopolized. In such a market, the monopolist is able to manipulate price, quantity, and quality to extract monopoly profits. Section 2 of the Sherman Act condemns not only the unlawful acquisition of monopoly power, but also the abuse of monopoly power by a monopolist that achieved its market power unlawfully.

Monopolization

Unlawful monopolization consists of two elements: (1) possession of monopoly power in the relevant market, and (2) the purposeful acquisition or maintenance of that power through exclusionary, abusive, or predatory practices.[78] In other words, the existence of monopoly power, whether legally or illegally acquired, and conduct that indicates an intent or purpose to exercise that power, amounts to monopolization. As with Section 1 claims, market power for monopoly claims under Section 2 is measured by reference to a relevant product market and a relevant geographic market.

A health care organization that has the ability or power to control prices or exclude competition has monopoly power. To prove the existence of monopoly power, it is not necessary to demonstrate that prices have actually been manipulated or that competitors have actually been excluded. Rather, mere possession of the power to do these things is sufficient proof of monopoly power.

The existence of monopoly power may be inferred when market share statistics indicate the relative dominance of a particular health care organization in the marketplace.[79] Although the precise market share percentage required to prove the existence of monopoly power varies according to differences in markets, courts have consistently determined that market shares of 70 percent to 90 percent are sufficient to establish the presence of a monopoly.[80] In *United States v. Aluminum Co. of America,*[81] the Second Circuit created the widely accepted rule of thumb that while a 90 percent market share is enough to constitute monopolization, "it is doubtful whether 60 or 64 percent would be enough; and certainly 33 percent is not." In general, absent special circumstances, a defendant must have a market share of at least 60 percent before it can be guilty of monopolization.[82]

Although market share percentage may be the easiest measurement of monopoly power, it is certainly not the only indicator of monopoly power. Factors other than market share that potentially evidence monopoly power include:

- barriers to entry or expansion
- maintaining market share with an inferior product or service
- technological superiority resulting in cost advantages
- price leadership, and substantial economies of scale
- the relative size of competitors

- pricing trends and practices
- homogeneity of products[83]

Of these additional factors, the most significant to the evaluation of monopolization claims is the existence of barriers to entry because monopoly power cannot exist without some barriers that prevent others from entering the market when the monopolist or entity with high market share percentage attempts to raise prices above the competitive level.[84]

The Sherman Act does not prohibit the mere existence of a monopoly. To violate the antitrust laws, a monopolist must have acted purposefully to acquire or maintain such power. The intent required to establish monopolization need not be a specific intent to monopolize the relevant market, however; it may be nothing more than a general intent to act in a manner that results in acquiring or maintaining monopoly power.[85] Thus, the intent can be inferred from acts that constitute an illegal restraint of trade under the Sherman Act or from an anticompetitive merger. Moreover, courts generally infer intent even if the monopoly results from the natural and probable consequence of the conduct of business.[86]

Courts may infer an intent to monopolize if a health care organization with a substantial market share offers no grounds for its opposition to a competitor's application for a certificate of need, or they may infer an intent to exercise monopoly power if the health care organization sets rates for particular services below the organization's costs to provide them. Health care organizations also may be affected by monopolization in markets other than the market for health care services. For example, an intent to monopolize could be inferred if a dominant insurer requires that the health care organization not participate in a competing plan. The following paragraphs discuss some other types of activity that may give rise to monopolization claims against a health care organization with dominant market power.

Monopoly Leveraging

A possible monopolization claim that could be brought against a health care organization is that it has engaged in "monopoly leveraging"—that is, the use of monopoly power in one market to obtain a competitive advantage in a second market. The Supreme Court has broadly stated that "the use of monopoly power, however lawfully acquired, to foreclose competition, to gain competitive advantage, or to destroy a competitor, is unlawful."[87] Monopoly-leveraging claims are closely related to tying arrangements. [For a more detailed discussion, see Tying Arrangements.]

To prove a monopoly-leveraging claim, a plaintiff must show that a defendant-health care organization has monopoly power in one market and that it exercised that power to gain an advantage in another market. Even if there is no real threat that the health care organization would thereby monopolize the second market, it still could be held liable for using its power in one market as leverage against competition in the second market.

In one case involving monopoly-leveraging claims against a hospital, the Eleventh Circuit reinstated a jury verdict of $2.3 million in favor of the plaintiff, a durable medical equipment (DME) company.[88] The court held that the hospital, which was part owner of a private DME company that competed with the plaintiff, had engaged in unlawful monopoly leveraging when it used its monopoly power in one market to gain market share in another by other than competitive means. In reaching this conclusion, the court relied on evidence indicating that the hospital had adopted policies that excluded competing DME vendors from reaching its discharged patients, and had unduly influenced home health care nurses to recommend DME equipment sold by the hospital.

It is worth noting, however, that whether a monopoly-leveraging claim constitutes a Section 2 violation where the advantage gained in the second market is something short of a monopoly or attempted monopoly is a matter of considerable controversy. Although the most recent monopoly-leveraging decisions in the health care field have not shed light on this question,[89] at least one federal district court has granted summary judgment for the defendant-hospital on a monopoly leveraging claim, where there was no probative evidence that the hospital had gained an unfair competitive advantage in the downstream market.[90] Although not specifically addressing the issue of whether monopoly leveraging constitutes a distinct cause of action under Section 2, the court found persuasive a line of cases denying a separate cause of action, and concluded that the anticompetitive dangers that implicate the Sherman Act are not present when a monopolist has a dominant market share in one market and uses its power to gain a competitive advantage in a second market.

Essential Facilities

Another area of antitrust concern for health care organizations possessing dominant market power in the relevant market is the potential for a plaintiff to claim that the organization's refusal to deal constitutes a violation of Section 2 of the Sherman Act under the "essential facilities" doctrine, which concerns a monopolist's use of a monopoly position in one market to deny access to a needed service or good to its competitors in another market. Under this doctrine, courts have ruled that where it is economically infeasible for a monopolist's potential competitors to duplicate a facility controlled by the monopolist and needed to provide a product or service, the monopolist must make the facility available to the competitors on a nondiscriminatory basis.[91] Application of the essential facilities doctrine requires proof of the following factors:

- control of the essential facility by a monopolist[92]
- a competitor's inability practicably or reasonably to duplicate the essential facility
- denial of the use of the facility to a competitor
- the feasibility of providing access to the facility[93]

Although the doctrine has been considered in many cases involving physicians challenging the revocation or denial of hospital privileges, the doctrine was intended for use in cases addressing a very different antitrust problem: a monopolist's exclusion of competitors from a "downstream market" by means of denying access to the essential facility.[94] With the increasing development of provider-based integrated delivery systems, antitrust risks have increased in this area. In recent years, providers that have been excluded from a particular health care network have brought monopolization claims based in part on the argument that due to the network's denial of access, the provider has been denied access to a "facility" essential to its ability to compete in the health care market.[95] In these cases, to show that an integrated delivery system or other health care network is an essential facility, an excluded provider must demonstrate that the exclusion caused it substantially more than inconvenience, or even some economic loss. The plaintiff attempting to establish a monopolization claim under the essential facilities doctrine must show that the exclusion constitutes a "severe handicap" that threatens to eliminate competition in the market for that service.[96]

Predatory Pricing

Predatory pricing occurs when a monopolist or would-be monopolist prices below its costs in the short run to drive competitors out of the market. The monopolist recovers these losses by charging monopoly prices in the future after the competitor withdraws from the market. Although the Supreme Court has addressed such claims without defining the standard for pricing below cost, it also has indicated a degree of skepticism toward predatory pricing cases involving competitive markets, noting the difficulties that the monopolist would likely encounter (in a market characterized by low barriers) in successfully raising *and maintaining* prices above the competitive level after driving out the competition. In such a market, the monopolist will be unable to recoup the short-term losses because other competitors will enter the market as soon as the monopolist attempts to raise prices. Nonetheless, predatory pricing is a well-recognized means of achieving or maintaining a monopoly position in violation of Section 2 of the Sherman Act, and in the health care context, at least one federal circuit court has addressed the appropriate analysis for defining this type of illegal conduct.[97]

Monopsony Power

Monopsony power refers to the power of a buyer to reduce the price of an input below the competitive price by restricting demand for the input. It is the mirror-image of monopoly power, and like monopoly, misallocates resources. It is analyzed under Section 2 of the Sherman Act. The most frequent targets of this type of claim in the health care realm have been Blue Cross/Blue Shield plans. Plantiffs in these cases frequently alleged that due to Blue Cross/Blue Shield's significant market power as a purchaser of hospital and physician benefits and services, it is able to extract favorable prices, at below competitive levels, from providers. Courts have generally rejected such arguments, however.[98]

EXEMPTIONS

There are a few situations in which actions that might otherwise raise antitrust concerns are exempt from antitrust scrutiny. For the most part, these circumstances involve dealings with the federal or state governments, but another potential exemption is applicable to activities that are considered to be the business of insurance or purely local in nature. In addition, if a health care organization is a nonprofit institution, it has a limited exemption from some of the prohibitions contained in certain antitrust laws.

The possibility that an exemption would apply should be examined whenever the action contemplated:

1. Is taken pursuant to federal law.
2. Is taken pursuant to state law.
3. Is taken pursuant to local government direction.
4. May be characterized as petitioning the government.
5. Involves the assumption or spreading of insurance risk.
6. Involves peer review decisions in furtherance of quality health care.

The following sections discuss these exemptions in greater detail.

Federal Immunity: Implied Repeal

In the health care sector, as well as in other industries, the federal government is immune from liability under the Sherman Act. This immunity extends to intermediaries and agents acting on behalf of the government. One type of federal immunity is the doctrine of implied repeal, which the courts have developed in recognition of the tension that exists between certain federal regulatory statutes and the federal antitrust laws. Under this exemption, action taken pursuant to a federal regulatory statute is exempt from antitrust scrutiny if application of the antitrust laws would irreconcilably conflict with the regulatory scheme. The implied repeal defense has been narrowly construed, however, and thus implied antitrust immunities are justified by only a clear showing of repugnancy between the antitrust laws and the regulatory statute. In fact, it has been held that any repeal should be implied only to the minimum extent "necessary to make the [statutory scheme] work."[99]

Hospitals frequently made use of this defense in connection with the health planning process when the National Health Planning and Resources Development Act (NHPRDA) was in effect.[100] This defense, however, was severely limited by a Supreme Court decision holding that the NHPRDA "is not so incompatible with antitrust concerns" that it completely repeals antitrust laws as applied to every action related to the health planning process.[101] Even after the repeal of the NHPRDA, some health care providers in antitrust cases have attempted to use the implied repeal exemption by arguing that the legislative history behind the NHPRDA indicates Congress' intent to repeal antitrust laws with respect to active participation in the development of health policy. The Ninth Circuit found such an argument unpersuasive, however, holding that the NHPRDA did not impliedly repeal antitrust laws in respect to such activities of health care providers, and more specifically, that antitrust laws apply to hospitals in the same manner that they apply to all other sectors of the economy.[102]

Application of the implied repeal exemption in one other context, Medicare, should be of interest to health care organizations. At least one federal court has ruled that a Medicare regulation that permits hospitals to engage in the group purchasing of supplies as a form of prudent buying does not irreconcilably conflict with the antitrust laws, and that the regulation did not exempt a hospital purchasing group from compliance with the antitrust laws.[103]

State Action Immunity

State and local governments' authority to regulate various private business and economic activity emanates from their police power to impose reasonable restrictions on private action in the interest of promoting public health, safety, and general welfare. Sometimes state and local regulation restricts or restrains competition, however, and this results in a conflict between governmental regulation and the antitrust laws. The state action doctrine, developed by the courts, grants an exemption, otherwise referred to as state action immunity, from antitrust sanctions whenever the defendants' anticompetitive conduct is the consequence of certain types of governmental regulation. The following sections discuss the courts' application of the state action doctrine to four different categories of activity involving health care entities: (1) actions taken by state agencies, (2) actions taken pursuant to state law, (3) peer review activities, and (4) hospital collaborative ventures covered by state statutes.

Actions Taken by State Agencies

It has long been held that the antitrust laws apply to private organizations, not to governments. This policy reflects the balance between the federal government's promotion of free competition and the principles of federalism that leave to the states the power to deal with particular local problems. Thus, actions taken directly by the states are immune from the antitrust laws. Local subdivisions of the state and other state agencies and "municipalities," however, are not automatically immune from antitrust liability unless their allegedly anticompetitive acts are authorized by the state. Only when such entities are acting pursuant to a "clearly articulated and affirmatively expressed" state policy to displace competition with regulation in a particular industry does anticompetitive conduct qualify for this type of immunity, more commonly known as immunity under the state action doctrine.

In the health care context, entities such as public hospitals are not considered to be "state" actors; even to the extent that a public hospital may be acting as a government agency, its connection to the state is tenuous enough to preclude its being characterized as the state for purposes of this antitrust exemption.[104] Rather, the courts generally have concluded that public hospitals are municipalities for purposes of the state action doctrine.[105] Accordingly, unless the challenged activity is specifically authorized by the state legislature (i.e., taken pursuant to state law, as discussed in the next section), alleged anticompetitive conduct of public hospitals may not be found exempt as state action.[106]

Actions Taken Pursuant to State Law

Private behavior that is regulated by the state may also be exempt under the state action doctrine. In 1985, the Supreme Court decided two important cases concerning this aspect of the doctrine. In *Town of Hallie v. City of Eau Claire,*[107] the Court ruled that when a municipality acts anticompetitively pursuant to a clearly articulated state policy, active state supervision is not a prerequisite to exemption from the antitrust laws under the state action doctrine. Alleged anticompetitive conduct is within the scope of a state's clearly articulated policy when it is a "foreseeable result" of state legislation, the Court held. In *Southern Motor Carriers Rate Conference v. United States,*[108] the Court ruled that the actions of a private party need not be compelled by state law to be exempt from the antitrust laws under the state action doctrine. The Court rejected the argument that only if the anticompetitive acts of a private party are compelled can a state's policy be "clearly articulated" so that the state action doctrine may apply. Instead, it ruled that a state policy that permits, but does not compel, anticompetitive conduct may be clear articulation within the meaning of the state action doctrine.

In the Supreme Court's most recent decision addressing the state action doctrine, *Federal Trade Commission v. Ticor Title Insurance Co.,*[109] the Court clarified the test for state action immunity by holding that affirmative steps must be taken by state authorities to satisfy the "active supervision" requirement. The case involved the FTC's challenge against the collective rate-making activities of title insurance rating bureaus in several states. The Court concluded that the facts did not establish "active supervision" where the rates established by a state-licensed rating bureau became effective unless the state rejected them. An active supervision analysis asks whether the state has played a substantial role in determining the specifics of the economic policy at issue. In this case, the state was not actively involved in overseeing the fees set for title insurance, and thus the rating bureaus were not immune from antitrust liability under the state action doctrine. Even after the *Ticor* decision, however, there is considerable uncertainty as to whether state regulatory review meets the standard set by the Court, and it remains a question of fact that must be answered on a case-by-case basis.

These Supreme Court cases have been cited in several health care decisions in a variety of contexts, as will be discussed in the following sections. The Fifth Circuit, for example, held that a public hospital's exclusive contract granting one physician the authority to provide chronic dialysis services at the hospital's end-stage renal disease (ESRD) unit falls under state action immunity based upon state certificate-of-need (CON) laws pertaining to ESRD facilities and laws authorizing hospitals to contract with any individual for the provision of such services.[110] Determining that the requirements of the state action doctrine had been met, the court reasoned that the alleged anticompetitive conduct was a foreseeable result of a statutory scheme that allows hospitals to enter into exclusive contracts with individual physicians to operate their ESRD units, and that protects existing ESRD facilities against competition by prohibiting hospitals from establishing such facilities without first obtaining state CON approval.

The state action doctrine has also been applied in the area of hospital mergers and acquisitions. More specifically, the doctrine has been found to exempt such transactions where one party is a political subdivision of the state, such as a governmental hospital authority or public hospital. Relying on *Town of Hallie,* the Eleventh Circuit held that a health care authority's proposed acquisition of a private health care facility was immune from federal antitrust liability because a state statute authorized it to acquire health care facilities.[111] A year later, the same Circuit held that the state action doctrine immunized from the FTC's antitrust scrutiny a Florida public hospital's acquisition of another local hospital because the state foresaw the possible anticompetitive effects of a state law authorizing public hospital boards to expand hospital facilities if necessary.[112] Noting that the board could not build a new facility because market conditions would not justify the issuance of a CON by the state, the court concluded that the only means to expand the facilities of the board-owned hospital was through acquisition. The court therefore reasoned that the state statute at issue gave the board implicit power to acquire other hospitals, and that such anticompetitive conduct was a foreseeable consequence of delegating such power to the board.[113]

Peer Review Activities

Numerous courts have relied on *Town of Hallie* and *Southern Motor Carriers* in determining whether the state action doctrine immunizes from antitrust scrutiny state-mandated actions of a medical staff peer review committee. In these cases, typically a physician has charged his or her competitors with an unlawful conspiracy by manipulating the peer review process. However, the Supreme Court has twice rejected arguments that state supervision of the peer review process gives rise to state action immunity.[114] In *Patrick v. Burget,* for example, the Court ruled that physicians in Oregon are subject to federal antitrust scrutiny for their activities on hospital peer review committees because the state does not actively supervise the peer review process.[115] Under the state action doctrine, the Court explained, anticompetitive conduct of private parties can be deemed state action and therefore be exempt from antitrust laws if the challenged restraint is clearly articulated and affirmatively expressed as a state policy and is actively supervised by the state. In Oregon, the state health department licenses hospitals, which are under a statutory obligation to establish and maintain peer review procedures, but the statutory scheme does not establish a state program of active supervision of peer review decisions. This kind of review fails to satisfy the state action doctrine's requirement of active supervision and thus the physician's conduct is subject to scrutiny under the antitrust laws, the Court held.

There have also been numerous cases at the lower federal court level addressing whether the peer review process in a particular state is protected from antitrust scrutiny under the state action doctrine. The results have been varied, but courts generally have rejected this defense. In one case, for example, the Third Circuit held that the state action doctrine did not protect a hospital's peer review activities in a case involving the hospital's decision to revoke the staff privileges of a urologist based on indications of professional incompetence and unprofessional conduct.[116] Because there is no state government actor that exercises ultimate authority over the actual merits of privilege determinations, there is no "active supervision" of hospital peer review activities, and thus they are not immune from federal antitrust liability, the court held. Other courts have reached essentially the same conclusion.[117]

Although in the minority, at least one federal district court has been able to rely on state peer review statutes in holding that peer review activities conducted by publicly owned hospitals are shielded from antitrust liability under the state action doctrine.[118] In this case a federal district court in Georgia rendered a decision, later affirmed by the Eleventh Circuit, that held that state action immunity applied to county hospital officials' decision to deny orthopedic surgical staff privileges to an osteopathic physician because the state clearly and affirmatively articulated a policy to displace competition with regulation in regard to public hospitals' peer review processes. The denial of staff privileges, according to the hospital, was based on the physician's failure to complete an approved orthopedic surgery training program to become eligible for certification by the American Board of Orthopaedics, as required by the hospital's bylaws. In determining that the hospital and its officials were immune from antitrust liability, the court relied upon state statutes that authorized the creation of hospital authorities with the ability to conduct peer review and credentialing, establish standards and procedures for the revocation of staff privileges, and protect professional health care providers from all criminal and civil liability for their participation in peer review activities. When the state enacted this statutory scheme, the court reasoned, it "reasonably anticipated" that local hospital authorities might act in an anticompetitive fashion in denying staff privileges based on the recommendations of their peer review committees.

State Statutes: Hospital Collaborative Ventures

A recent development in the health care field that affects the applicability of the state action doctrine to mergers and acquisitions involving private hospitals is the enactment in many states of statutes that expressly exempt mergers, acquisitions, and other transactions among hospitals from state antitrust laws if the parties can establish that the consumer benefits of the transactions exceed any harm to reduction in competition. The intent behind such statutes is to facilitate cooperative endeavors or mergers between hospitals or other health care providers.[119] If such statutes call for state oversight, these transactions may also be exempt from federal antitrust scrutiny under the state action doctrine. Whether, and under what circumstances, state action immunity will apply is not always clear, however, the Supreme Court has not yet addressed the issue of state action immunity in the specific context of private hospital mergers.

Although only a few actual exemptions have been reported under these statutes, state attorneys general are increasingly investigating hospital merger transactions. In North Carolina, for example, a proposed "partnership" between a medical center and a hospital to effect the merging of selected services was approved by the state following the entities' compliance with the process set out in the state Hospital Cooperation Act, which allows hospitals to enter into cooperative arrangements without being subject to antitrust scrutiny if they first obtain a certificate of public advantage.[120] Before issuing the certificate, the state imposed specific criteria relating to pass-through cost savings, increased access, and health maintenance.

More recently, the Montana attorney general's office conditionally approved, under its antitrust exemption statute,[121] the merger of the only two hospitals in Great Falls, Montana; both hospitals were private parties. Issuance of a certificate of public advantage by the state DOJ was conditioned upon various restrictions and requirements, including limitations on the amount of revenue the merged hospitals can receive from patients and a related requirement that cost savings be passed on to consumers in the form of price reductions; required participation in a state-administered program for monitoring health care quality; required construction of additional inpatient operating rooms; required adoption of guidelines on patient referrals so as not to deny competitors access to potential customers; and the required submission to the state of an annual report containing information on resulting efficiencies.[122]

It should also be pointed out that during the past five years, hospital merger transactions in at least five other states have been handled by the state, although not through a process established by statute (as in the cases described previously), but through a consent-decree process.[123] In Maine, for example, a state court approved a consent agreement between the state attorney general and four private hospitals in adjacent communities regarding a proposal to integrate the hospitals' respective PHOs into a single contracting network (sometimes referred to as a "super-PHO").[124] In proposing the formation of the super-PHO, the four separate PHOs sought immunity under Maine's Hospital Cooperation Act, which grants exemptions to hospitals that can prove that any anticompetitive effects resulting from their collaborative ventures are outweighed by community benefits (e.g., reduction in health care costs, improved quality, and access to services). Under the consent agreement, the super-PHO will allow its member hospitals and physicians to participate in other networks and managed care plans; create financial incentives, such as fee withholds; and accept capitated payment contracts and other at-risk payment schemes from payers. In addition, the attorney general's office will monitor the super-PHO's charges and utilization rates, and upon a finding of any anticompetitive results, will temporarily prohibit entering into new contracts.

Actions Taken Pursuant to Local Government Direction

The Local Government Antitrust Act of 1984[125] eliminates antitrust damage liability for the official conduct of a local government, its officials, or its employees in suits brought under Sections 4, 4A, and 4C of the Clayton Act. It also provides the same protection for persons acting pursuant to local governmental direction.

The Local Government Antitrust Act was found to be a bar to an antitrust suit against a county hospital by a physician who was denied certain medical staff privileges.[126] The physician contended that the local government exception is narrow, and does not apply to county hospitals. The federal trial court rejected that view, finding that the county acts through the hospital to provide for the welfare of its citizens. It concluded that the hospital's acts are the acts of the county, and are therefore immune from antitrust challenge.

Another court held that a hospital district is a "local government" within the meaning of the Local Government Antitrust Act and is therefore absolutely immune from liability for damages under the Clayton Act.[127] In a Fourth Circuit case, a corporation that managed a county hospital was found to be immune under the Act for its decision not to renew an emergency department services contract.[128] Another case held that a city health care authority that operates a hospital is protected from antitrust challenge under both the Local Government Antitrust Act and the state action exemption.[129]

The Noerr-Pennington Doctrine

Concerted attempts by hospitals to influence units or instrumentalities of state or federal government to obtain legislation, redress, or other favorable action are ordinarily exempt from antitrust scrutiny under the Noerr-Pennington doctrine. Like the state action exemption, the Noerr-Pennington doctrine represents an effort to reconcile conflicts between the antitrust laws and certain other principles of our legal system; the principle in question is the constitutionally protected right of citizens to petition the government for redress of their grievances. The doctrine thus provides broad protection for that right, holding that attempts to influence governmental action may be challenged under federal antitrust law in only the rarest of circumstances.

Courts have held exempt under the Noerr-Pennington doctrine allegedly anticompetitive activities that consist of no more than legitimate lobbying efforts by a particular group of health care providers. In a case involving ambulance services, for example, the Eighth Circuit held that the Noerr-Pennington exemption applied to successful lobbying by the owners of four ambulance companies that had consolidated into one corporation, resulting in a citywide plan to create one ambulance service system.[130] There are numerous other cases involving health care providers that demonstrate the extent to which the Noerr-Pennington doctrine protects efforts to secure governmental action, even where facts plainly indicate an anticompetitive purpose and effect.

Noerr-Pennington protection is not unlimited, however. If the activity is not a genuine effort to influence a government action, but is an attempt to interfere directly with a business relationship of a competitor, or has the primary purpose of depriving competitors of meaningful access to an agency or court,[131] it may be characterized as a "sham."[132] Moreover, an activity may be characterized as a sham if competitors otherwise abuse the government system (e.g., commit perjury), even if the relief sought is otherwise legitimate.[133]

In the health care context, another important exception to the Noerr-Pennington doctrine is that it does not apply to the government in its role as a purchaser of health care services. In a commercial transaction such as one where the government is purchasing health care services, any conduct that would be considered a violation of antitrust law as applied to a private purchaser is not protected simply because a governmental entity is involved. Thus, in at least one case involving the government as a customer of health care services, a federal court has held that price-fixing relating to government contracts or concerted refusals to deal with governmental entities are not protected simply because they involve communications with government.[134]

Nonprofit Institutions

The FTC Act grants a limited exemption from unfair competition claims to nonprofit institutions that are solely charitable enterprises. Like all antitrust exemptions, the nonprofit institution exemption has been narrowly interpreted. To claim this exemption, a nonprofit organization must be charitable in both form and fact; in other words, the exemption extends only to nonprofit corporations that are organized for and are actively engaged in charitable activities.[135] In this context, organizational purposes other than those of a charitable, educational, civic, health, welfare, scientific, or research orientation will be suspect.

Significantly, organizations operated for both exempt and nonexempt purposes will probably not be exempt.[136] The exemption will not be extended to a nonprofit corporation, such as a trade association, that carries on some business activities for its own profit or for the profit of its members. In *American Medical Association v. Federal Trade Commission,*[137] for example, the exemption was not extended to the American Medical Association (AMA), a nonprofit organization, because it has both business and nonbusiness objectives. The AMA lobbies in support of legislation for the profit of its members and renders business advice to its members.

The exemption is provided for under statutory language known as the Non-Profit Institutions Act;[138] this statute provides that nonprofit institutions, even if not solely charitable within the meaning of the FTC Act, enjoy an exemption from the Robinson-Patman Act[139] for "purchases of their supplies for their own use." The Supreme Court enunciated the limits of the term "own use" for consumable supplies in *Abbott Laboratories v. Portland Retail Druggists Association,*[140] which discusses several categories of sales and dispensations of pharmaceutical products by hospitals. The Court characterized dispensations to patients (inpatients, outpatients, or emergency department patients) for use on the hospital's premises as part of the institution's basic function and, therefore, considered them to be for the hospital's own use. In addition, the Court considered to be for the hospital's own use: prescriptions given to patients upon discharge for their personal use for a limited time as a continuation of the treatment that had been administered at the hospital and dispensations to hospital employees, students in hospital programs, or physician members of the staff for their personal use or for the use of their dependents. Discounts granted to the hospital for these uses were, therefore, held to be within the exemption. The Court determined that refills of former patients' prescriptions and prescriptions given to persons who are not hospital patients are not for the hospital's own use and therefore are excluded from the exemption.

In subsequent cases, the Supreme Court and lower federal courts have addressed the application of the "own use" rule to other nonprofit entities. In *Jefferson County Pharmaceutical Association v. Abbott Laboratories,*[141] for example, the Supreme Court ruled that state and local government hospitals are subject to the same restrictions as other nonprofit hospitals in the resale of discounted pharmaceutical products. Thus, the Court concluded that the sale of pharmaceutical products to these governmental hospitals for resale in competition with community pharmacies is not exempt from the Robinson-Patman Act. Two years later, in *DeModena v. Kaiser Foundation Health Plan, Inc.,*[142] the Ninth Circuit ruled that an HMO's purchase of low-cost drugs for resale to its members does not violate federal antitrust law. The court cautioned, however, that sales made to walk-in customers who are not HMO subscribers are not exempt.

As hospitals and other health care organizations move into related markets, such as long-term care, home health, and ambulatory surgicenters, new issues may arise concerning the applicability of the exemption. In part because of increasing concerns about the anticompetitive effects of pharmaceutical resale schemes usually involving nonprofit hospitals, HMOs, or other health care entities, Congress enacted the Prescription Drug Marketing Act (PDMA),[143] which prohibits hospitals and other health care entities that are not drug wholesalers or licensed retail pharmacies from reselling prescription drug products; the statute provides criminal penalties for violations.

For nonprofit health care organizations considering the use of the nonprofit institution exemption as a defense in an antitrust lawsuit, one other caveat regarding the exemption's scope is worth noting. The exemption does not provide a means of escaping the FTC's jurisdiction over transactions that fall under that agency's regulatory authority. In recent cases, federal courts have held that the FTC has jurisdiction to regulate nonprofit hospitals under Section 7 of the Clayton Act. [144]

Business of Insurance

The McCarran-Ferguson Act[145] establishes an exemption from the federal antitrust laws for actions that constitute the "business of insurance," to the extent such business is regulated by state law; thus, the primary purpose of the McCarran-Ferguson Act is to allow states to regulate the activities of insurance companies. To qualify for the exemption, the anticompetitive practices (1) must be part of the business of insurance; (2) must be regulated by state law; and (3) may not take the form of coercion, intimidation, or boycott.

The Supreme Court has identified criteria that determine whether a challenged activity is the business of insurance. In *Group Life and Health Insurance Co. v. Royal Drug Co.*,[146] the Court held that a Blue Shield agreement with participating pharmacies that allowed policyholders to purchase prescription drugs at reduced prices did not constitute the business of insurance. In examining this arrangement, the Court noted that (1) the pharmacy agreements did not spread any risk, but merely arranged for the purchase of goods and services; (2) the agreements did not constitute an integral part of the relationship between the insurer and the insured; and (3) the pharmacies were parties wholly outside the insurance industry. Thus, if an agreement, such as a health plan participation agreement, neither defines nor spreads risk, but merely specifies or minimizes the insurer's costs, the agreement will not be an exempt activity within the business of insurance. Subsequent to the *Royal Drug* decision, the Supreme Court and lower federal courts have held that various aspects of the relationship between health care providers and insurers are not protected by the McCarran-Ferguson Act, and are therefore subject to antitrust scrutiny.[147]

The development of health care financing alternatives to traditional fee-for-service insurance products has further reduced the protection that insurers have under the McCarran-Ferguson exemption. In *Reazin v. Blue Cross and Blue Shield, Inc.,*[148] the Tenth Circuit held that activities of Blue Cross and Blue Shield that served the purposes of economically injuring a hospital as a warning to other health care providers who might enter into a relationship with Blue Cross competitors is not exempt from antitrust scrutiny under the McCarran-Ferguson Act. The court therefore permitted antitrust claims relating to attempted monopolization of a broad "health care financing" market that included Blue Cross/Blue Shield's business of traditional insurance products as well as its business as a third-party administrator for self-insured firms.

As application of the McCarran-Ferguson exemption in this area is still evolving, the question of whether the conduct of health insurance companies qualifies for the exemption in markets for new products that are replacing traditional fee-for-service insurance must be resolved on a case-by-case basis. From the case law that has been generated in this context thus far, however, it appears that insurers do not enjoy protection under the McCarran-Ferguson Act in connection with most aspects of their relationship with health care providers. Health care organizations should recognize that the exemption may not serve as an adequate protection from antitrust liability in many cases, including matters such as:

- the negotiation and implementation of fees, discounts, and the terms and conditions of contracts for physician services
- the refusal of an insurer to deal with a particular provider or group of providers
- utilization and quality control activities

This inapplicability of the McCarran-Ferguson exemption to most aspects of the insurer–provider relationship is a benefit to health care organizations because it protects them from anticompetitive conduct on the part of insurance companies, but on the other hand, it also potentially subjects these organizations' dealings with insurance companies to heightened antitrust scrutiny.

Health Care Quality Improvement Act

The Health Care Quality Improvement Act of 1986 (HCQIA)[149] was enacted partially as a response to numerous antitrust suits against participants in peer review and credentialing activities. Congress passed the Act to encourage continued participation in these activities. The purpose of the HCQIA is to provide those persons giving information to "professional review bodies" and those persons assisting in review activities limited immunity from damages that may arise as a result of adverse decisions that affect a physician's medical staff privileges. Immunity does not extend, however, to civil rights litigation or litigation filed by the United States or a state attorney general. The Act also establishes a mandatory reporting scheme for information relating to physician competence.

Entities covered by the immunity provisions of HCQIA include hospitals as well as entities that provide health care services and professional societies if those entities or societies engage in formal peer review activities intended to promote the quality of care. The immunity provision, however, applies only if the following requirements have been satisfied:

- The challenged peer review action must have been taken in the reasonable belief that the action was in the furtherance of quality health care.
- The action must have been taken after reasonable efforts to obtain the facts of the matter.
- The entity must have afforded the affected physician adequate notice and hearing procedures, as specified in the statute.
- There must be a reasonable belief that the action was warranted.

The HCQIA creates a presumption that these requirements have been satisfied, which can only be rebutted by a preponderance of the evidence.

Perhaps because of the numerous conditions that must be met to obtain valid HCQIA immunity, there has been a relatively slow increase in the number of antitrust cases involving a defendant-health care organization seeking such immunity in relation to claims that peer review activities constituted illegal anticompetitive conduct. In 1992, the Ninth Circuit was the first appeals court to consider application of HCQIA immunity to a staff privileges action; it ruled that a physician peer review committee had met all the due process requirements under HCQIA and was therefore shielded from antitrust liability.[150] Since then, the cases in this area are growing, and other federal and state courts have also granted HCQIA immunity to the peer review activities of hospitals and physician participants in the peer review process.[151]

In an Eleventh Circuit case, for example, the court overturned a $4.2 million jury award for a disciplined surgeon whose staff privileges were terminated on the basis of disruptive behavior, finding that the hospital's peer review action had satisfied all conditions for HCQIA immunity.[152] After a series of disciplinary problems related to abusive treatment of hospital staff by the surgeon, the hospital terminated the surgeon's privileges. Subsequently the surgeon sued, alleging various state and federal antitrust law violations. In reversing a jury's judgment in favor of the surgeon, the appeals court noted that

HCQIA carries a presumption in favor of immunity, and that therefore the surgeon must prove that the peer review process was not reasonable. That burden of proof was not met in this case, the court concluded, finding that evidence presented did not overcome the presumption that the hospital acted in furtherance of quality care, and reasonably made the determination that the surgeon's termination was warranted by the circumstances.

At least one state court, however, has held that a hospital was not entitled to a presumption that its peer review activities were conducted in furtherance of quality care under a state statute similar to the federal HCQIA.[153] A cardiologist filed a complaint with the state medical board after his privileges were terminated by the only hospital in his area. The board reversed the termination, and the hospital appealed to the state court, contending that its peer review activities were cloaked with a presumption in favor of immunity. Although such a presumption is not expressly provided for in the relevant state statute, the hospital argued that it is implied because many of the statute's provisions parallel the federal HCQIA. Refusing to extend HCQIA's presumption to state law, the court emphasized that the federal HCQIA applies to liability actions against peer reviewers and not to appeals of state agency actions. Further, even though the state legislature intended the state law to be consistent with HCQIA, the court concluded that failing to adopt HCQIA's presumption did not create an inconsistency.

One significant issue that has been debated in a few antitrust cases involving claims of HCQIA immunity is whether HCQIA, if its provisions are complied with, insulates hospital and health care professionals from litigation, as well as from liability. At least two federal circuits have held that HCQIA provides immunity from damages, but not from suit; in other words, peer review participants are shielded from liability for their action, but not from the trial process itself.[154] These courts found persuasive legislative history behind HCQIA indicating that a provision granting a right to be free from trial was initially considered when the legislation was drafted, but a congressional committee expressly deleted the provision upon its conclusion that such broad protection might be abused and used as a shield for anticompetitive economic actions.

CONTRACTS AND OTHER AGREEMENTS

Although particular joint practices, such as mergers, are covered specifically by the Clayton Act, the antitrust risk of most joint activities must be determined under the Sherman Act. For the most part, however, the factors considered in connection with the analysis of the antitrust implications of contracts and other agreements are the same under either the Sherman Act or the Clayton Act.

Agreements Related to Price

The legality of any agreement related to price depends largely on the nature of the parties to the agreement. Although horizontal agreements among competitors likely will be analyzed under the per se rule, many vertical arrangements between sellers and buyers are permissible under the rule of reason.

Horizontal Agreements on Price

Horizontal agreements between competitors relating in any way to price have long been recognized as per se violations of the Sherman Act. Even if the agreement affects the pricing mechanism only indirectly, the agreement is illegal, because "the machinery employed by the combination for price fixing is immaterial."[155] Prohibited activities in this area include not only straight "price fixing" but also any collusive activity among competitors that has the effect of raising, depressing, pegging, or stabilizing the price of a commodity.[156]

Moreover, a horizontal agreement among competitors is per se illegal even if the prices agreed upon are reasonable. As the Supreme Court stated in *United States v. Socony-Vacuum Oil Co.*, an agreement will be characterized as price fixing

> [i]f the range in which purchases or sales will be made is agreed upon, if the prices paid or charged are to be at a certain level or on ascending or descending scales, if they are to be uniform, or if by various formulae they are related to the market prices. They [prices] are fixed because they are agreed upon.[157]

Thus, price fixing includes joint action to set minimum or maximum prices, as well as any agreement that tends to stabilize prices. [For a more detailed discussion of health care cases involving joint action to set minimum or maximum prices or to stabilize prices, see Fee Schedules, and Relative Value Scales discussed next.]

Other arrangements that affect price less directly, such as agreements on bidding, limiting production, and advertising prices, also have been characterized as per se illegal price fixing. In one interesting health care case involving advertising, for example, the Second Circuit held that a provision within the AMA's Code of Medical Ethics that restricted physicians from advertising constituted an unlawful restraint on competition in violation of Section 5 of the FTC Act.[158] In so holding, the court reasoned that the effect of the ban was to deprive consumers of information about the availability of health care services, to deter the offering of innovative forms of health care, and to stifle alternatives to delivery of services, including alternative payment options.[159]

Fee Schedules

Establishment of maximum or minimum fee schedules by competitors clearly falls within the prohibition against price fixing. The case of *Arizona v. Maricopa County Medical Society*[160] involved two foundations for medical care (FMCs) that had been organized by medical societies to promote fee-for-service medicine and to provide the community with a competitive alternative to existing health insurance plans. The foundations allowed their physician members to establish the maximum fees that a physician could claim in full payment for health services provided to policyholders of FMC-sponsored insurance plans. Arizona Attorney General sued the foundations on the ground that such arrangements constituted price fixing and were, therefore, per se unlawful under the Sherman Act. The Supreme Court, in a four-to-three decision, held that the maximum fee schedules established by the FMCs were per se illegal under the antitrust laws. In its opinion, the Court rejected the contention that procompetitive justifications for the fee arrangements made the per se rule inapplicable. The Court also noted that the physicians were not required to set the prices. Rather, the Court suggested that the insurance companies should have this power.

Reimbursement policies of insurance companies also have been challenged as illegal price-fixing agreements, and in cases wherein there is evidence of provider control over reimbursement insurance, the courts generally have shown interest in reviewing such claims.[161] When providers exert minimal control over reimbursement policies, however, courts have generally been unreceptive to antitrust suits against insurance companies based on claims that their reimbursement policies constitute illegal price fixing.[162]

One case in this area is particularly interesting because it is one of the few criminal enforcement actions based on price-fixing charges against health care professionals brought by the DOJ in recent years. The agency charged three dentists among a group of dentists with illegal horizontal price-fixing through actions they undertook after a series of meetings where the group complained about low co-payments for dental services provided to beneficiaries of certain managed care plans.[163] Following the meetings, the defendants, as well as other dentists, mailed form letters that suggested fee schedules that would incorporate higher co-payments to the plans; the plans ultimately did increase the co-payment level. A jury convicted all three defendants, but the trial court reversed the conviction as to two of the defendants and granted a new trial as to the third defendant. On appeal, however, the Ninth Circuit reversed and reinstated the convictions, based on its conclusion that the dentists' joint presentation of a fee schedule to third-party payers did indeed constitute per se illegal price fixing. Even though the dentists lacked the economic power to force insurer compliance, such lack of power was irrelevant under the per se rule, the court explained. Observing that it could be lawful for the dentists to meet and discuss "commiserating over low fee schedules" or even to "band together to negotiate various other aspects of the relationship with the plans such as payment procedures," the court nonetheless concluded that the dentists could not lawfully engage in joint negotiation of formulas or levels of pricing.

The Antitrust Division of the DOJ has indicated less willingness to tolerate discussions between competitors that revolve around fee schedules or pricing levels in any way. Circumstances implying any form of collusion on price, including the discussion of current fee schedules, have been targeted in civil antitrust enforcement actions. There are numerous cases, many of which have been settled by consent decree, that demonstrate the antitrust agencies' clear disapproval of joint discussions or negotiations regarding formulas or levels of pricing, even when a specific price is not jointly discussed. In one case, for example, 22 obstetrician/gynecologists practicing in counties surrounding Savannah, Georgia, entered into a consent decree with the DOJ under which they were barred from discussions about adopting uniform, increased, or specific fees, and from communicating with competitors in any way about current or future fees.[164]

Health care organizations are thus well advised to exercise extreme caution and to obtain legal counsel with respect to any circumstances involving price discussions with competitors. Although participating providers in health care networks should be able to engage in general discussions related to the marketplace, including the development of new managed care programs or the entry of new managed care plans into the market, discussions that in any way touch on private payer-specific price proposals are best avoided.

Relative Value Scales

To arrive at equitable reimbursement rates for medical practitioners, some insurers and other payers have adopted a relative value scale, a system for comparing the complexity of various medical procedures. For example, setting a fracture may have a relative value of 3 units, while removing an appendix may have a relative value of 10 units. The appropriate reimbursement is determined by applying a conversion factor to the relative value. If the conversion factor is $30 per unit, reimbursement for setting a fracture in the preceding example would be $90; reimbursement for an appendectomy would be $300.

Because relative value scales relate to the establishment of prices, they could be characterized as per se violations. The Court's decision in *Maricopa* does not necessarily require that result, however. The FMCs in *Maricopa* had developed both a relative value scale and a conversion factor.[165] In contrast, the American Society of Anesthesiologists developed and circulated a relative value scale without a conversion factor. In *United States v. American Society of Anesthesiologists, Inc.,*[166] the only reported case in which the court specifically considered this circumstance, the court found no evidence that the relative value scale was intended as anything other than a suggested method for arriving at appropriate fees or that any third party was coerced into accepting them. Rather, the court found that the relative value scale was merely a logical starting point for negotiations with insurers and did not constitute price fixing.

Both the FTC and the DOJ have, on occasion, challenged the legality of the development and circulation of relative value scales by physician organizations. Prior to the *Anesthesiologists* decision, the FTC initiated several actions against professional societies that had developed relative value scales, alleging that these scales had the effect of "establishing, maintaining, or otherwise influencing the fees" charged by physicians. In each reported case, the FTC obtained consent orders by which the societies agreed to withdraw their relative value scales and to refrain from developing any such scale in the future.[167] Also prior to the *Anesthesiologists* decision, the DOJ obtained a similar consent order in at least one other action against a professional society that had developed a relative value scale.[168]

An FTC advisory opinion to the American Society of Internal Medicine, issued approximately five years after the *Anesthesiologists* decision, contains the most detailed and current explanation of the FTC's view of medical society dissemination of relative value scales.[169] The case involved the medical society's proposal to develop relative value scales that it would request that payers consider in formulating reimbursement programs. The society also proposed sending a report to physicians and third-party payers that would explain how to use the relative value scales to reduce the disparity between reimbursement rates for cognitive and procedural services. In its advisory opinion, the FTC commented that an agreement in restraint of trade would likely be found if a professional association advised marketplace conduct to its members or their competitors, and the intent or likely result of such communication was that the recipients of the disseminated data would engage in concerted or interdependent action to modify their rates. There likely would be no agreement in restraint of trade, however, if an association merely provided information or advice that could be used by recipients unilaterally, and there was no intent or likelihood of resulting concerted activity, the FTC explained. As for the facts at issue, the FTC did not approve the proposed conduct based upon its conclusion that it posed a danger of interdependent adherence to the relative value scales.

Since the issuance of this opinion, neither agency has indicated any change in its position regarding the dissemination of relative value scales, and thus it would be prudent for a professional organization to seek clearance before developing and disseminating a relative value scale.

Discounts

Because a discount is a component of price, concerted action to establish uniform discounts is likely to be characterized as per se illegal price fixing. In *Catalano, Inc. v. Target Sales, Inc.,*[170] the Supreme Court held that an agreement among beer wholesalers to eliminate the practice of extending interest-free credit on purchases by retailers was per se illegal. The Court explained:

> It is virtually self-evident that extending interest-free credit for a period of time is equivalent to giving a discount equal to the value of the use of the purchase price for that period of time. Thus, credit terms must be characterized as an inseparable part of the price. An agreement to terminate the practice of giving credit is thus tantamount to an agreement to eliminate discounts, and thus falls squarely within the traditional per se rule against price fixing.

Nevertheless, in some cases, such as establishing reimbursement mechanisms in relation to contractual arrangements between insurance companies and participating providers, uniform discounts are not likely to be subject to the per se rule.

In *Royal Drug Co. v. Group Life and Health Insurance Co.,*[171] for example, the Fifth Circuit held that a prepaid drug insurance program that involved separate but uniform agreements between Blue Shield and several Texas pharmacies and that entitled Blue Shield policyholders to obtain prescription medications for a nominal price does not constitute a per se antitrust violation. The court found that because Blue Shield does not compete with any participating pharmacy there was no unlawful agreement among competitors to fix prices. In essence, the court reasoned, the parties "sit on opposite sides of the bargaining table," and Blue Shield has rightfully bargained for the best deal it could get.

In the context of managed care, similar reasoning has been extended to the establishment of reimbursement mechanisms in contractual arrangements between managed care plans and participating providers. It is widely accepted that a managed care plan has the right to seek to contract with physicians on the plan's proposed compensation terms. "Selective contracting" by PPOs, HMOs, and other private insurance plans is generally acceptable behavior from an antitrust perspective; in other words, such entities can approach physicians or a physician organization and propose "take it or leave it" compensation terms, usually without offending antitrust laws. Accordingly, managed care plans often seek, and obtain, significant discounts from physicians' standard prices on a fee-for-service basis, or in the alternative, an agreement to accept some other payment scheme such as capitation. In a discounted fee-for-service arrangement, a managed care plan and a participating provider or group of providers agree on a percentage discount from the providers' customary fee schedule as a compensation mechanism.[172]

Thus, for the managed care plan concerned about antitrust risk, establishing uniform discounts from physicians' standard prices is a much wiser course of action than establishing fee schedules; such discounts eliminate many of the price-fixing evils articulated in *Maricopa,* in which all the providers charged the same fee according to an established schedule. One caveat applies to both uniform discounts and fee schedules, however: any evidence of concerted action among competitors in establishing these components of price can present a significant degree of antitrust risk.

Horizontal Agreements on Price among Purchasers

As a matter of antitrust theory, agreements among purchasers with respect to price, otherwise known as group purchasing arrangements, should be analyzed much as agreements among sellers are analyzed. Nevertheless, courts treat the two types of agreements very differently, often applying the rule of reason to buying agreements. Because the courts recognize that group purchasing of goods and services can promote competition and may result in substantial efficiencies to individual members of the purchasing group as well as the vendors, the antitrust analysis is modified such that market power is a factor that may determine whether there will be per se condemnation of a buying arrangement. As the Supreme Court stated in *Northwest Wholesale Stationers, Inc. v. Pacific Stationery and Printing Co.*,[173] "wholesale purchasing cooperatives . . . are not a form of concerted activity characteristically likely to result in predominant anticompetitive effects," while further explaining that economic efficiencies resulting from such arrangements typically allow smaller retailers to compete more effectively with larger retailers.

In the context of health care, courts and the antitrust enforcement agencies have found group purchasing agreements to be lawful based on potential efficiencies and lack of significant buyer market power. In a case involving hospital group purchasing, for example, the Sixth Circuit reversed the lower court's decision finding unlawful a group purchasing arrangement between a hospital cooperative and a national distributor of medical and surgical supplies under which the cooperative received volume discounts, and held that such an arrangement did not violate antitrust laws.[174] In a similar case, a federal district court in Georgia held that a group purchasing agreement between a hospital cooperative and a vendor of hospital forms was not a per se violation.[175] Declining to apply the per se rule to the case, the court noted that a "group purchasing arrangement is a conventional means of reducing costs to participating members," and concluded that, absent evidence relating to market power, such an arrangement was not an unlawful restraint on trade.

Perhaps persuaded by the reasoning in these cases, at least one state—Rhode Island—has passed a statute exempting from its antitrust laws joint purchasing activities of health planning services.[176] The intent of the statute is to "improve the efficiency with which health care services are rendered and curb the increasing rates of health care costs," and thus it expressly permits health care facilities to enter into agreements that provide for group planning, individual or group expenditure ceilings, allocation of services or specialties, group purchasing, and shared services arrangements.

Nonetheless, if group purchasing arrangements are not properly structured, they can raise antitrust concerns, especially when the arrangement represents purchasers that collectively can exercise market power in their purchases. Additionally, courts will be suspicious of group purchasing arrangements that may be used to restrict price competition, divide markets, boycott suppliers, or unreasonably exclude other interested buyers from the purchasing group. Courts have condemned as per se violations certain group buying activity; typically such cases have involved agreements among purchasers that the courts have found to be nothing more than attempts to fix the purchase price of goods below competitive levels.[177]

Unlike such "sham" buying arrangements (i.e., where the actual purpose of the arrangements is price fixing), the underlying motive behind most group purchasing arrangements involving health care organizations is to promote efficiencies in some way. Thus, in the health care context, courts and the antitrust agencies have consistently viewed these arrangements as potentially procompetitive and deserving of analysis under the rule of reason. Moreover, hospital buying groups in the market for hospital supplies will very rarely possess market power,[178] and absent market power, such cases usually receive rule-of-reason treatment.

Nonetheless, if a hospital buying group faces a challenge to a buying arrangement on antitrust grounds, it should be prepared to demonstrate some procompetitive effects. It may be prudent to identify significant resulting efficiencies, such as lower transaction costs and economies of scale, before entering into such an arrangement. Moreover, hospitals must ensure that there is no potential for even the appearance that the buying group is being used to engage in anticompetitive acts. If the court suspects that a group arrangement of buyers is being used for anticompetitive purposes such as fixing resale prices or driving competitors out of the market, it will be much more likely to apply the per se standard. To better understand how the DOJ and the FTC analyze these arrangements, hospitals should become familiar with the agencies' *1996 Policy Statements;*[179] one of the nine statements therein specifically pertains to joint purchasing arrangements among health care providers. [For a more detailed discussion, see Joint Purchasing Arrangements.]

Vertical Agreements on Price Between Buyers and Sellers

Contracts between a buyer and a seller, which establish a price for the goods or services purchased, generally will be analyzed under the rule of reason. This does not include, however, vertical price-fixing agreements, which will be analyzed under the per se standard. One form of vertical price fixing that falls squarely within the category of per se illegality is known as *resale price maintenance;* this term refers to an agreement between the buyer and seller that fixes the price at which the buyer will resell the product, a practice that has the anticompetitive effect of depriving the consumer of price competition with respect to the particular product.

In the health care context, federal courts have considered antitrust claims alleging unlawful resale price maintenance or other price-fixing schemes in cases involving prepaid subscription drug programs where the defendant-insurance company has entered into contractual arrangements with participating pharmacies. Typically under such arrangements, each participating pharmacy provides prescription drugs at stipulated prices, generally lower than current charges, to uninsured customers. In *Royal Drug Co. v. Group Life and Health Insurance Co.,*[180] for example, a group of independent pharmacists in Texas argued that the fixed dispensing fee in their contracts with a third-party plan constituted per se illegal price fixing because it was a form of resale price maintenance. The pharmacists argued that third-party plan enrollees were analogous to consumers harmed by a resale transaction in which the price is essentially maintained by the third-party plan. The Fifth Circuit disagreed, concluding that the fixed dispensing fee in the pharmacy agreements was not a form of resale price maintenance and that therefore the per se rule did not apply to the facts of the case. The third-party plan is the purchaser in this case and the pharmacy agreements were no more than "arrangements for the purchases of goods and services," the court reasoned, and therefore there was no resale transaction. In applying the rule of reason to the pharmacy agreements, the court found in favor of the third-party plan in light of the pharmacists' failure to present any evidence of anticompetitive effect.

In another case, the Ninth Circuit held that pharmacy agreements implementing a third-party plan's prepaid prescription drug plan did not constitute per se illegal price fixing because the agreements did not control "any sale other than the one between the insurance company and the pharmacy."[181] Price fixing constituting per se illegal conduct, the court explained, is an agreement to fix prices to be charged to third parties, not between the contracting parties themselves. Thus, agreements between a purchaser (insurance company) and seller (pharmacy) are not the sort of price-fixing agreements that violate the antitrust laws because such agreements do not set prices charged to third parties. The court ultimately upheld the agreements, concluding from its rule-of-reason analysis that they did not fix prices charged to parties outside the agreement.[182]

Courts have extended this reasoning to cases involving insurance participation plans—that is, agreements between physicians and insurance plans (such as Blue Cross/Blue Shield), under which the physicians provided services to plan participants at fixed rates. In one case, for example, the Seventh Circuit ruled that a voluntary incentive program offered by Blue Cross/Blue Shield, in which participating physicians were reimbursed by the insurance company at a price based on the company's "usual, customary, or reasonable" payment policies, does not constitute price fixing.[183] The court held that Blue Cross/Blue Shield was merely acting as a purchaser of medical services on behalf of its subscribers and that the reimbursement program constituted a legitimate contract between buyers and sellers of medical services.

Similarly, the Ninth Circuit found no antitrust violations with respect to agreements between physicians and Blue Cross/Blue Shield that not only set the reimbursement rate for certain services, but also obligated the participating physicians to notify patients of this arrangement if a referral was made to a nonparticipating physician.[184] Although acknowledging that these vertical agreements had the effect of foreclosing nonparticipating physicians from doing business with patients insured under the Blue Cross/Blue Shield plan, the court concluded that such foreclosure was an "ordinary consequence of every commercial contract," and thus held that the agreements did not violate antitrust laws because they did not impermissibly distort the market.

Most-Favored-Nation Clauses

It seems clear that a most-favored-nation provision should be evaluated under the rule of reason. In this arrangement, a health care organization or physician is obligated to provide services to a particular purchaser at a price no less favorable than that at which it provides services to its most favored customer. In the context of health plans and networks, a most-favored-nation clause is a requirement, usually in a provider agreement, that participating providers charge other plans or networks at least as much as they charge the network or plan implementing the most-favored-nation clause. Because most-favored-nation provisions do not tend to affect physicians' decisions about the level of their fees, courts have consistently declined to characterize such provisions as per se illegal price fixing.

In *Associated Milk Dealers, Inc. v. Milk Drivers Union, Local 753,*[185] the Seventh Circuit expressly rejected the plaintiff's claim that a most-favored-nation clause was per se illegal. Rather, the court held that such a clause violates the antitrust laws only if it has a predatory purpose and an anticompetitive effect. Similarly, in *Blue Cross and Blue Shield v. Michigan Association of Psychotherapy Clinics,*[186] a most-favored-nation clause was found not to be illegal price fixing, because there was no intent to fix prices charged to third parties and no interference with the freedom of providers to fix their own fees.

The First Circuit has ruled that a Blue Cross HMO's "prudent buyer" policy, under which physicians were paid no more than they would accept from any other health care payer for a given procedure or service, did not constitute monopolization in violation of Section 2 of the Sherman Act.[187] The court decided that the most-favored-nation clauses employed by Blue Cross constituted a legitimate effort by Blue Cross, as a purchaser of health care services, to get the best possible price for the services it purchases and were aimed at the legitimate goal of keeping costs down. That fact, combined with Blue Cross's lack of market power, made the prudent buyer policy lawful.

In a more recent court decision involving Blue Cross/Blue Shield's monopoly claims against a health care network, the Seventh Circuit described the most-favored-nation clause as a procompetitive device by which payers "try to bargain for lower prices, by getting the seller to treat them as favorably as any of their other customers . . . the sort of conduct that the antitrust laws seek to encourage."[188] Both the Antitrust Division of the DOJ and the FTC were concerned that this language would be read as suggesting that most-favored-nation clauses are always legal, and thus the agencies were among numerous parties that filed amicus briefs suggesting reconsideration of the court's statement in this area. The court subsequently modified its opinion, noting the possibility that under some circumstances, most-favored-nation clauses can have anticompetitive effects.

Despite numerous court decisions upholding most-favored-nation provisions, in recent years the federal antitrust agencies have shown an active interest in challenging the use of these provisions in agreements between health plans and participating providers under certain circumstances. In general, such circumstances include a high percentage of providers in a defined market (e.g., dental insurance) participating in a health plan that implements the most-favored-nation clause, and revenues from that plan accounting for a significant percentage of the participating providers' revenues. Under this market scenario, the most-favored-nation clause can inhibit both the entry of new plans into the market as well as the growth of competing plans, and also can preclude providers from offering price discounts.

In *United States v. Delta Dental Plan of Arizona, Inc.*,[189] for example, the Antitrust Division of the DOJ and the Arizona Attorney General challenged the use of most-favored-nation clauses by a dental insurance plan that contracted with businesses, government agencies, and other organizations to provide dental care services to the employees of those entities. The plan was the dominant dental provider in the relevant market, with approximately 85 percent of all dentists in the state providing services for the plan. Moreover, most of the participating dentists received a substantial percentage of their income as a result of revenues from services rendered under the plan. In their complaint, the federal agency and state attorney general's office alleged that the dentist-controlled plan conspired with others to eliminate discounts and reduce price competition for dental services. Given the circumstances, the effect of the most-favored-nation clauses in provider agreements was to make it too costly for participating dentists either to discount fees below those offered by the plan or to terminate their participation in the plan. In reaching a settlement by consent decree, the plan agreed to eliminate the clauses from its participating provider agreements, and to cease from engaging in any other action that might limit future fee discounts for dental services. Similar results were obtained in other agency enforcement actions brought in 1995 and 1996.[190] Also, at least one other state has pursued health care networks using most-favored-nation provisions in their agreements.[191]

In a more recent case, the Antitrust Division of the DOJ challenged a most-favored-nation clause used by a dental plan in Rhode Island. Although this case raised many of the same issues that were considered in prior enforcement actions, it differed in a very significant way: it was not terminated by a consent decree prior to being litigated in court. Instead, upon a motion to dismiss from the defendant-dental plan, a federal district court denied such request, and rendered an opinion expressly rejecting that case precedent establishes a per se rule of legality for most-favored-nation clauses.[192] Although the case was subsequently settled by consent decree under which the dental plan agreed to eliminate such clauses from its provider contracts, the court's ruling remains significant in that it may indicate a more receptive view among courts in general with respect to the antitrust agencies' approach to analyzing most-favored-nation clauses imposed by health plans that have a large share of the relevant insurance market, and that contract with a large percentage of providers in a defined market for health care services.

Balance Billing

Participation agreements with insurers that set levels of reimbursement below the health care organization's usual charges may contain provisions that prohibit the organization from billing covered patients for the difference between charges and the amount of reimbursement. Such bans on balance billing protect the insurer's subscribers from costs that they did not anticipate and should be permissible in most cases. In *Kartell v. Blue Shield,*[193] for example, the First Circuit held that a ban on balance billing imposed by an insurer with a dominant market share and virtually unanimous participation by physicians did not unreasonably restrain trade. The court viewed the insurer as a purchaser of physicians' services for its insured, rather than as a "third force" preventing willing buyers and sellers from independently reaching price/quality agreements. The court ruled that the insurer's use of monopoly power to obtain "lower than competitive" prices did not violate Section 2 of the Sherman Act because the law is aimed at "protecting consumers against prices that were too high, not too low," and because a legitimate buyer is entitled to use its market power to keep prices down.

In another case, a group of hospital-based radiologists alleged that an insurer's requirement that contracting hospitals include radiology services as a part of the package of services provided to subscribers, combined with the insurer's ban on balance billing, constituted both a concerted action in restraint of trade under Section 1 and monopoly leveraging, illegal under Section 2.[194] The court dismissed the Section 1 claim on the basis that the antitrust laws do not prohibit a buyer from specifying that the services it buys on the account of others must be fully paid services. The Section 2 claim was dismissed because the evidence did not support the monopoly leveraging claim. The court commented that even if the insurer had used market power to obtain favorable prices, the law does not prevent a buyer with market power from negotiating a good price or specifying what it will buy.

Market Allocation

Arrangements that allocate portions of the market among competitors are typically viewed as per se illegal.[195] Thus, any agreement to direct patients to particular hospitals or other health care entities based on geographical location, services required, or a method of payment may be characterized as per se illegal market allocation. Moreover, competitors cannot lawfully agree that one will not open offices in the other's "territory" or not compete in another's territory.[196] Also, an agreement among competing hospitals that one will provide cardiac care, one will provide orthopedic care, and so forth, or that only one will seek a CON to obtain a computerized axial tomography scanner, would probably be considered illegal market allocation.

Market allocation that is ancillary to an otherwise legitimate arrangement may be permitted. For example, joint ventures effectively allocate the market among participants. If the joint venture enables the participants to enter a new market that they would not have entered by themselves, the arrangement will often be permitted. If it appears that market allocation is a principal goal of the venture, however, the arrangement will be held to be per se illegal.

In the health care context, allocations with respect to "on-call" schedules and use of hospital facilities have been found to be unlawful division of markets. In one recent case, for example, the Maine state attorney general's office obtained a consent decree from five obstetrician/gynecologists who were alleged to have decided among themselves to allocate the availability of the gynecological operation room at the hospital where they practiced.[197] More specifically, the obstetrician/gynecologists had agreed to adopt a block booking system for the scheduling of operations, which resulted in their having exclusive access to the operating room at particular times of the week. According to the complaint, this agreement precluded other physicians from starting or expanding their surgical practices, and therefore constituted an unlawful market allocation.[198]

Because an agreement among competing physicians with regard to on-call schedules and access to hospital facilities may be subject to antitrust scrutiny based on claims of illegal division of markets, hospitals should consider adopting policies that specify clearly that on-call schedules for services (e.g., hospital-based physician coverage, emergency department coverage, etc.) are to be determined by a hospital representative (e.g., administrator or medical director) who neither is a participant (competitor) in the call schedule, nor has a financial interest that would tend toward favoring one group of physicians over another.

Group Boycotts or Concerted Refusals To Deal

Although any single entity may unilaterally refuse to deal with any other business, the refusal becomes unlawful when two or more entities so agree. For example, in *St. Paul Fire and Marine Insurance Co. v. Barry,*[199] the Supreme Court found that an agreement of three insurers not to deal with the policyholders of a fourth insurer constituted an unlawful boycott because it compelled those policyholders to accept reduced medical malpractice coverage.

Traditionally, all group boycotts have been considered inherently anticompetitive and, therefore, characterized as per se violations of the Sherman Act. In *Northwest Wholesale Stationers, Inc. v. Pacific Stationery and Printing Co.,* the Supreme Court identified three characteristics as indicative of per se illegal boycotts:

1. The boycott cuts off access to a supply, facility, or market necessary to enable the victim firm to compete.

2. The defendant possesses a dominant market position.
3. The practices are not justified by plausible arguments that they enhance overall efficiency or competition.[200]

Exclusions in the health care context, however, are not necessarily reviewed under the per se rule. According to the First Circuit:

> . . . per se condemnation is not visited on every arrangement that might, as a matter of language, be called a group boycott or concerted refusal to deal. Rather, today that designation is principally reserved for cases in which competitors agree with each other not to deal with a supplier or distributor if it continues to serve a competitor whom they seek to injure. . . . We doubt that the modern Supreme Court would use the boycott label to describe . . . a joint venture among competitors in which participation was allowed to some but not all . . . although such a restriction might well fall after a more complete analysis under the rule of reason.[201]

Reazin v. Blue Cross and Blue Shield, Inc.[202] is one of the few cases in which the court has found sufficient market power to support a per se group boycott claim. In that case, a jury found that Blue Cross and Blue Shield of Kansas (Blue Cross) had devised a scheme to economically injure a hospital as a warning to other providers who might enter into a relationship with Blue Cross competitors. Blue Cross and several area hospitals conspired to exclude a particular hospital from participation in the Blue Cross plan. The hospital was affiliated with a managed care plan that competed with Blue Cross. A jury returned a multimillion dollar award in favor of the excluded hospital. This verdict was affirmed, given Blue Cross's market power, the evidence of conspiratorial conduct, and the anticompetitive reduction of competition.

In recent years, an increasing number of courts have reached the conclusion that vertical agreements between a physician (or physician group) and a managed care organization (or hospital) not to deal with a third party are subject to the rule-of-reason antitrust analysis. In one case, for example, an independent laboratory and a radiology clinic sued an HMO that refused to contract with them, alleging that such conduct constituted a concerted refusal to deal.[203] The Oregon Supreme Court ruled, however, that under the per se approach, the HMO does not have market power or unique access to a business element necessary for effective competition in the laboratory and radiology markets. Therefore, the threshold showing that the HMO's actions were per se illegal had not been made. Turning to the rule of reason, the court found that rather than suppressing competition, the HMO actually increased it. In addition, the HMO's share of the market was so small that any overall anticompetitive effect was questionable. The court therefore concluded that the HMO's refusal to contract with the providers was not illegal.

In another case involving exclusion of a radiology group from an independent practice association (IPA), the Second Circuit held that "defendants' type of exclusivity practices are vertical, nonprice restraints that [must be] analyzed not under the per se rule, but under the 'rule-of-reason' standard."[204] The appeals court determined that an agreement among physician members of an IPA to exclude a group radiology practice so that its own radiologists could exclusively serve patients enrolled in the HMO for which the IPA provided services did not violate federal antitrust law because the agreement did not harm competition, and because the IPA possessed insufficient market power to potentially lessen competition.

Courts generally recognize that managed care organizations must operate in a cost-effective manner. Exclusion of practitioners because of their failure to do so appears to be legitimate. In one case, for example, a legitimate joint venture's decision to exclude two allergists who had failed to render care in a cost-effective manner was found not to constitute an illegal group boycott.[205] In any event, the IPA lacked the market power necessary to find a violation of the Sherman Act. As a general rule, a practitioner or group of practitioners excluded from a physician-based joint venture (IPA, PPO, PHO, or other form of joint venture—e.g., equipment, clinical, group purchasing, etc.) is unlikely to prevail on a claim of illegal group boycott or concerted refusal to deal unless the participants in that joint venture collectively dominate the local market for physician services. Such market power is also an essential element to establishing an illegal group boycott claim based on the denial, termination, or suspension of a physician's staff privileges.[206]

It is also generally recognized that, assuming no concerted activity that may affect a naked restraint of trade, a health care practitioner or group of practitioners can determine how much it will charge for its health care services as well as terms related to the sale of such services. Indeed, absent extraordinary circumstances (e.g., emergency procedures), a practitioner can refuse to sell services unless the purchaser of such services (e.g., a third-party payer) reaches a contractual arrangement with the practitioner on the terms of sale for those services. Although this scenario involves a vertical agreement that likely will be subject to the rule of reason, a concerted refusal to deal with a payer may give rise to antitrust liability. In *FTC v. Indiana Federation of Dentists,*[207] for example, the Supreme Court applied the rule of reason to a boycott by dentists of insurance companies' requirements that patient X-rays be submitted in conjunction with insurance claims forms for reimbursement and found the practice to be illegal. The dental association had adopted an aggressive campaign urging dentists not to submit X-rays to insurers in order to force them to review the X-rays in the dentists' offices. Because the dentists had not expressly agreed that they would not sell their services to insurers and because the dental association urged that the X-ray policy was adopted for quality of care purposes, the Court did not apply the per se rule. Under a "quick-look" rule-of-reason analysis, the boycott was nonetheless illegal, the Court held, emphasizing the clearly anticompetitive effects of the boycott as well as the association's failure to establish any procompetitive justification for refusing to deal with the insurance companies.

Even under the current, more flexible approach toward certain group boycotts, however, a concerted refusal to deal that results in a naked restraint of trade (i.e., when it has no possible legitimate justification) is still likely to be condemned as a per se violation. Examples of concerted activities that have been condemned as per se illegal include:

- taking action to drive out existing competitors
- attempting to monopolize a market
- fixing prices

- enforcing retail price restrictions that implement territorial allocations
- increasing a seller's market dominance
- engaging in predatory practices

More recently, physician threats to boycott other providers based on the potential that such providers may negatively impact physician(s)' competitive or economic circumstances also have been subject to antitrust scrutiny. In one case, for example, the FTC alleged that certain members of a hospital's medical staff had agreed to boycott the hospital to induce the hospital to cease operation of a multispecialty clinic that would provide extended hours of service and other benefits for patients.[208] The defendant-staff members informed the hospital that a group of physicians would withhold patient admissions and encourage other physicians to participate in their boycott, according to the FTC complaint. Although the defendants argued that their discussions with the hospital were conducted on an individual basis and thus constituted unilateral decisions rather than concerted action, the FTC found in favor of the hospital and approved a consent decree based on charges of concerted refusal to deal.[209]

Tying Arrangements

Tie-ins, or tying arrangements, involve a seller's refusal to sell one product (called the "tying product") unless the buyer also purchases a different product (called the "tied product"). Sellers may require such an arrangement to increase sales of the tied product through their leverage in the market for the tying product, to discriminate in the price of the tying product, to decrease distribution costs through package pricing, or to preserve the good will associated with the tying product by requiring the use of a high-quality complementary product. Not all tying arrangements are illegal. If two products are sold together because there is not demand for one separate from the other, or if tying regulates and promotes competition rather than destroying it, the tie-in will survive judicial scrutiny.[210]

The rationale for proscribing tying arrangements is that they enable a seller to exert leverage in one market to increase sales in another. As stated in *Siegel v. Chicken Delight, Inc.*,

> [t]he hallmark of a tie-in is that it denies competitors free access to the tied product market, not because the party imposing the arrangement has a superior product in that market, but because of the power or leverage exerted by the tying product.[211]

In essence, "the vice of tying arrangements lies in the use of economic power in one market to restrict competition on the merits in another."[212]

The legality of tying arrangements is determined through a four-factor test. To be considered unlawful, the arrangement must:

1. Relate to two separate products or services.
2. Enable the seller of the tying product to coerce purchase of the tied product.
3. Involve a not insubstantial amount of interstate commerce in the tied product.
4. Create anticompetitive effects in the tied market.[213]

Each of these factors must be evaluated individually to determine whether a particular tying arrangement is unlawful. An arrangement that meets these tests is per se illegal, regardless of any procompetitive justifications.

For health care organizations, allegations of illegal tie-ins could occur in connection with purchasing arrangements or shared services arrangements. In addition, conditioning the availability or desirability of operating room time on the lease of office space in a hospital-owned building could potentially be characterized as a tie-in. Finally, exclusive agreements can arise in charges of anticompetitive conduct under a tying theory.[214] In *Jefferson Parish Hospital District No. 2. v. Hyde,*[215] for example, the plaintiffs claimed that an exclusive contract between a hospital and an anesthesiologist group was unlawful as a tying arrangement, making it per se illegal if it foreclosed a substantial share of the market. According to the plaintiffs, the contract violated antitrust law's prohibition against tying because as a result of that contract every patient who underwent surgery in the hospital had to use the services of one of the anesthesiolgists from the contracting group. The facts also revealed that 30 percent of patients residing in the relevant geographic area used the hospital. The Supreme Court refused to hold that the hospital's exclusive contract was a per se illegal tying arrangement, even though finding that anesthesiological services constitute a product separate from other hospital services and therefore subject to analysis as a tie-in. Nonetheless, the hospital's 30 percent market share standing alone did not demonstrate sufficient economic power to "force" patients to utilize the services of the anesthesiologist group, and therefore, the Court reasoned, the arrangement is not subject to condemnation under the per se rule. Ultimately, the Court upheld the exclusive agreement under a rule-of-reason analysis, finding the market share percentage insufficient to demonstrate an unreasonable restraint of trade. [For a more detailed discussion of antitrust analysis with respect to exclusive agreements, see Exclusive Agreements, discussed next.]

Exclusive Agreements

In response to increased competition and managed care, health care organizations are more frequently using exclusive agreements to obtain better services, higher quality goods, greater efficiency, and lower prices. As the use of these exclusive arrangements has proliferated, challenges to their legality by disgruntled competitors have increased.

To determine whether an exclusive agreement is permissible, it is necessary to consider its effect on competition, as well as market characteristics and business justifications.[216] Market share is the most probative factor in this analysis, and courts vary the weight given to other factors according to the market share involved. When the market share foreclosed is small, other measures of market performance are more likely to be weighed to determine the overall effect of the restraint on competition. Similarly, when the market foreclosure is neither clearly de minimis nor clearly significant, the courts focus on other factors, including any proffered justifications, to determine the legality of the exclusive arrangement.

Generally, the shorter the duration of the exclusive arrangement, the more likely that it will be upheld.[217] In contrast, the longer the term of the exclusive arrangement, the more likely that the arrangement's restrictiveness will be found to outweigh any business efficiencies or legitimate benefits it produces.[218]

Further, the economic justifications for an exclusive dealing arrangement must be evaluated to determine whether the arrangement promotes or suppresses competition. In most cases, health care organizations have multiple justifications for such agreements; for example, exclusive arrangements could (1) benefit patients by reducing costs and making quality control more effective, (2) enhance competition among local providers of health care services, or (3) result in better and more efficient services. Courts may also inquire into whether a less restrictive alternative could accomplish the same purpose as the exclusive arrangement.[219] If the exclusivity requirement is not reasonable in light of the competitive problems it was designed to meet, a court is likely to find it unlawful.

In the health care context, exclusive arrangements have typically been held unlawful only when they result in substantial foreclosure of the market,[220] and in the absence of a showing of anticompetitive effects, often have been permitted. In one case, for example, the Seventh Circuit relied on the absence of evidence indicating anticompetitive effects in ruling that a hospital's staffing decision to terminate its contract for anesthesia services with a business owned by three registered nurse anesthetists, and to enter into an exclusive contract for such services with an independent physician anesthesiologist, is not an exclusive agreement in violation of the Sherman Act.[221] The nurse anesthetists alleged that the competing physician-anesthesiologist had the intention to hurt their business when he billed hospital patients and third-party payers for anesthesia services he had not performed, and contacted local physicians to convince them that the nurse anesthetists' billing rate was excessive. Subsequent to such activities, the hospital terminated its contract with the nurse anesthetists, opting for an exclusive contract with the physician. The court found no violation of the Sherman Act, reasoning that the nurse anesthetists had failed to show that the hospital's staffing decision had an impact on competition within the relevant market, and therefore there was no antitrust injury. Concluding that the nurse anesthetists' allegations were insufficient to establish an antitrust claim, the court observed that the antitrust laws are not intended for circumstances where the plaintiffs claim no more than an exclusion from practicing in their preferred business form, and where evidence indicates little to no anticompetitive effect.

Courts that have applied the traditional analysis of exclusive agreements to exclusive hospital-physician arrangements have uniformly upheld the arrangements because their benefits were found to outweigh the economic harm they caused.[222] The procompetitive purposes that have been advanced for exclusive arrangements include:

- Improved efficiency in the operation of the service
- Promotion of control and standardization of procedures
- Better scheduling economy and availability of services
- Better supervision and training techniques
- Improved monitoring to ensure that medical standards are met
- Enhancement of the hospital's reputation, which enables the hospital to attract the most qualified
- Participation in the hospital's educational program
- Better use of equipment
- Greater commitment by physicians to the institution
- Specialization in certain techniques

These factors are balanced against any anticompetitive purposes and the competitive harm caused to determine the reasonableness of an exclusive agreement. Thus, a health care organization can attempt to reduce its antitrust risk in this area by establishing and documenting the sound business justifications for the exclusive dealing agreement. The existence of legitimate business reasons usually is considered by both the courts and the antitrust enforcement agencies in their rule-of-reason analysis of exclusive-dealing claims.

Joint Action in Relation to Contract Negotiation

Joint action with respect to issues that are not antitrust-sensitive should be evaluated under the rule of reason. The benefits of joint action on matters unrelated to price, territories, quantity, and perhaps quality may outweigh any potential harm. The primary justification for joint action with regard to certain issues is that it provides contract uniformity and ease of administration. Indeed, when a single purchaser (third-party payer) or vendor desires to enter into a series of bilateral agreements with hospitals, the single entity may find it desirable to deal with the hospitals as a group. Assuming that this choice is made freely by the single entity and the negotiations are not coercive in any way, the cost savings achieved by joint negotiation may outweigh any anticompetitive effect.

Under the rule of reason, the facts of each particular case must be considered. With respect to several types of provisions, joint negotiation does not ordinarily expose a health care organization to significant risk. However, as these matters approach antitrust-sensitive issues, such as price, caution must be increased. Also, in the managed care context, a managed care plan's nonprice contract terms may have the potential of resulting in an unlawful concerted refusal to deal. If the plan offers administrative terms, utilization controls, or other nonprice-related terms that are disagreeable to physicians, for example, a situation may arise in which physicians collectively refuse to deal unless the plan withdraws or modifies the objectionable terms. The Supreme Court found such conduct to be an unlawful concerted refusal to deal in one case involving a group of dentists who collectively refused to comply with an insurer's demand for copies of X-rays to be used by the insurer in evaluating claims.[223] The federal agencies also have specifically addressed this issue in their *1996 Policy Statements.* [For a more detailed discussion, see Safety Zone for Provision of Medical Information.]

Appointing a Collective Bargaining Agent

Appointing a collective bargaining agent to negotiate on behalf of a group of competitors, but without granting the agent authority to bind any member of the group, should not in itself violate the antitrust laws. In most cases involving collective negotiation, however, an antitrust violation has been found because some anticompetitive activity accompanied the bargaining process. Usually, the anticompetitive factor was associated with the inherently coercive nature of joint negotiations. Indeed, except when joint purchasing is necessary to obtain a volume discount, the threat of a collective refusal to deal is frequently the motivation for collective bargaining in the first place. Nevertheless, there is a narrow area of legality for collective negotiations that are unaccompanied by group coercion.[224]

Although courts do not necessarily infer from collective bargaining that an individual cannot exercise independent discretion in deciding whether to accept the terms of a collective bargaining agreement, both the FTC and the DOJ have taken somewhat stricter positions with regard to certain collective bargaining activities in the health care industry. In *In re Michigan State Medical Society,*[225] for example, the FTC considered a charge that a society of physicians had conspired with its members and component societies to fix physicians' fees. The medical society had established a negotiating committee that operated as its liaison with Blue Cross and Blue Shield. When controversy arose over a uniform claim and coding system, as well as over the use of a statewide screen to calculate reimbursement, the negotiating committee recommended that the members join in a concerted campaign to compel Blue Cross and Blue Shield to modify their position concerning these issues. As part of this campaign, physicians were asked to authorize the medical society, by proxy, to revoke a physician's participation in Blue Cross and Blue Shield; to refuse to submit the proper claim forms for services rendered to Blue Cross and Blue Shield subscribers; and to refuse to participate in "per-case" payments.

In finding the medical society's actions unlawful under a rule-of-reason analysis, the FTC focused on the specific actions taken to coerce Blue Cross and Blue Shield into accepting the medical society's position. The FTC order is particularly instructive concerning the scope of forbidden collective negotiation activities. It prohibited the medical society from:

- agreeing or attempting to agree with any of its members to affect the amount or calculation of reimbursement, including agreements to cancel participation or refuse to complete forms
- advocating that its members engage in such prohibited actions
- entering into or attempting to enter into any agreement with any third-party payer concerning reimbursement
- acting as an agent for any of its members in their dealings with third-party payers concerning reimbursement or in their acceptance or rejection of any participation agreement
- threatening any coercive acts by any of its members to compel any third-party payer to accept positions taken by the medical society or any of its members concerning reimbursement

Similarly, in a more recent case, the Antitrust Division of the DOJ reached a settlement agreement (via consent decree) with eight hospitals located in Long Island, New York, under which the hospitals were required to cease using a jointly formed organization as their exclusive bargaining agent for the purpose of contracting with HMOs and other managed care plans.[226] After forming such an organization, the hospitals collectively approved all the terms of their HMO agreements. In challenging the arrangement as violative of antitrust laws, the DOJ charged that the organization went far beyond mere assistance to each hospital in negotiating with HMOs and managed care plans. In particular, the organization facilitated the hospitals' collective agreement to include a provision in their contracts with HMOs that prohibited per diem pricing, which is a pricing mechanism directed at lowering hospital costs through improved patient management and shorter hospitalization. The consent decree prohibited the hospitals from using a joint organization for the purposes of agreeing with other hospitals on: the selection of contracting third-party payers, the terms of any fee or price term to a third-party payer, and the use of per diem-based fees in contracts. Moreover, the hospitals affiliated with the organization were barred from communicating any negotiated fee to another hospital in the region and from using the organization or any other agent to determine any hospital fees.

Thus, the federal antitrust enforcement agencies have indicated their disapproval of the formation of an organization to act as a collective bargaining agent on behalf of its members in their dealings with third-party payers and/or managed care plans concerning reimbursement or in their decisions to enter into participating provider contracts with such entities. [For a more detailed discussion of the agencies' view of collective negotiation in relation to fee-related terms, see Data Dissemination, and Safety Zone for Provision of Fee-Related Information discussed next.]

Data Dissemination

Mere exchange of data should not violate the antitrust laws. Indeed, as the Supreme Court stated in *United States v. United States Gypsum Co.*,

> [T]he exchange of price data and other information among competitors does not invariably have anticompetitive effects; . . . such practices can in certain circumstances increase economic efficiency and render markets more, rather than less, competitive.[227]

If, however, sharing of information leads to a price-fixing agreement or other unlawful behavior, the sharing of information itself would be prohibited.

In one recent case brought by the DOJ, for example, eight hospitals and two hospital associations in Utah were charged with violating the Sherman Act by conspiring to exchange wage information for the purpose of fixing registered nurses' compensation.[228] According to the agency's complaint, the hospitals and associations exchanged nonpublic, prospective, and current information about overall budgets, nursing budgets, and registered nurse entry wages, with the intention and effect of stabilizing registered nurse entry wages and limiting the amount and frequency of registered nurse entry wage increases in the relevant area. As a result of this information exchange, the agency argued, registered nurses in the area were deprived of the benefit of open competition in the market for registered nursing services, including smaller annual increases in the entry wage than the hospitals would have paid absent the information exchange. Following a three-year criminal investigation, the DOJ settled the case with the issuance of three consent decrees under which the hospitals and associations agreed to various prohibitions, including a ban on: agreeing to fix nurses' compensation or exchanging information concerning the current or prospective compensation paid to nurses, except in limited circumstances; and conducting or facilitating such information exchanges, except in specified circumstances. In addition, the decrees require the hospitals and associations to implement comprehensive antitrust compliance programs, and to submit annual written certifications showing compliance with the decrees.

The DOJ and the FTC have addressed this area in Statements 4 through 6 of their *1996 Policy Statements*,[229] which create safety zones that apply to data dissemination involving: (1) providers' collective provision of non-fee-related medical information to purchasers of health care services, (2) providers' collective provision of fee-related information to purchasers of health care services, and (3) hospital exchanges of price and cost information among providers. These statements are discussed in the sections that follow.

Safety Zone for Provision of Medical Information

The agencies' safety zone related to providers' provision of medical information to purchasers of health care services, as outlined in Statement 4, permits the collective provision of medical data that may improve purchasers' resolution of issues relating to the mode, quality, or efficiency of treatment. Thus, the agencies will not challenge, absent extraordinary circumstances, a medical society's collection of outcome data from its members about a particular procedure that they believe should be covered by a purchaser, and the provision of such information to the purchaser. The statement also covers the development of suggested practice parameters by providers within the safety zone. In providing medical data, providers may collectively engage in discussions with purchasers about the scientific merit of the data.

Specifically excluded from this safety zone, however, are any attempts by physicians to coerce purchasers to follow their recommendations. Moreover, providers who collectively refuse to deal with a purchaser because they object to the purchaser's administrative, clinical, or other terms governing the provision of services run a substantial antitrust risk. The policy also emphasizes that this safety zone applies only to information concerning practice-related matters.

Safety Zone for Provision of Fee-Related Information

A very different safety zone applies to the collective provision of fee-related information to purchasers. According to Statement 5, the collective provision to purchasers of factual information about providers' current or historical fees or other aspects of reimbursement, such as discounts or alternative reimbursement methods, are unlikely to raise significant antitrust concerns. To qualify for the safety zone, however, the collection of information to be provided to purchasers must satisfy the following conditions:

- the collection must be managed by a third party (e.g., a purchaser, government agency, health care consultant, academic institution, or trade association)
- although current fee-related information may be provided to purchasers, any information that is shared among competing physicians or that is available to the competing physicians furnishing the data must be more than three months old
- for any information that is available to the physicians furnishing the data, there are at least five physicians reporting data upon which each disseminated statistic is based; no individual physician's data may represent more than 25 percent of a weighted basis of that statistic; and any information disseminated must be sufficiently aggregated such that it would not allow recipients to identify the prices charged by any individual provider

According to the statement, the safety zone is intended to ensure that an exchange of price or cost data is not used by competing providers for discussion or coordination of provider prices or costs.

The statement also specifies certain activities that fall outside the safety zone, including collective negotiations between unintegrated physicians and purchasers in contemplation or in furtherance of an agreement among the providers on fees or other terms or aspects of reimbursement. Also excluded from the safety zone are agreements among unintegrated providers to deal with purchasers on only agreed terms.

Safety Zone for Exchanges of Price and Cost Information

The agencies' safety zone related to provider exchanges of price and cost information, as outlined in Statement 6, permits participation by competing hospitals in surveys of prices for hospital services, or of salaries, wages, or benefits of hospital personnel, if conducted pursuant to criteria set forth by the guidelines. The agencies will not challenge price or wage surveys that meet the following requirements:

- the survey is managed by a third party (e.g., a purchaser, government agency, health care consultant, academic institution, or trade association)
- the information provided by survey participants is based on data more than three months old
- there are at least five hospitals reporting data upon which each disseminated statistic is based; no individual hospital's data represent more than 25 percent on a weighted basis of that statistic; and any information disseminated is sufficiently aggregated such that it would not allow recipients to identify the prices charged or compensation paid by any particular hospital

According to the statement, these conditions are designed to ensure that the surveys are not used by hospitals to coordinate their competitive behavior.

Exchanges of price and cost information that fall outside the safety zone will be evaluated under the rule of reason; in other words, public, nonprovider initiated surveys (outside the safety zone) may be permissible if they do not create, on balance, undue anticompetitive effects. Nonetheless, the agencies still consider exchanges of future prices or future compensation anticompetitive. Moreover, if an information exchange also includes an agreement among competing hospitals to set or fix prices or wages, that agreement will be considered per se unlawful.

Development of a recommended methodology for disseminating data could raise related antitrust concerns because the methodology affects the competitive impact of the dissemination. For example, a methodology that provides a meaningful basis for comparison by consumers would tend to be more procompetitive than a methodology that does not and merely disseminates raw data. In addition, methodology that obscures significant data could be sufficiently anticompetitive so as to be an unlawful restraint in and of itself.

MERGERS AND ACQUISITIONS

Perhaps the most restrictive kind of joint activity is that which completely eliminates a competitor. Thus, corporate consolidations that unduly increase concentration in any market are held to violate the antitrust laws. Antitrust implications should, therefore, be considered whenever a health care organization is involved in a consolidation involving a merger, stock acquisition, or asset acquisition.[230]

Because a business consolidation has a direct impact on market concentration and an indirect impact on competition, the antitrust analysis of these transactions focuses on market concentration rather than actual effect. In most cases, the courts attempt to predict the anticompetitive effects that are likely to result from an increase in market share. Under the *DOJ/FTC 1992 Horizontal Merger Guidelines* (hereinafter *1992 Merger Guidelines*), however, the anticompetitive effects are presumed from market share increases.[231] [For discussion of market power, see Market Power, under Fundamental Antitrust Principles.]

Horizontal Consolidations

A horizontal merger involves similar or identical businesses at the same level of the market. There is no single qualitative or quantitative factor from which it can be determined whether such a merger is permissible. Recognizing a congressional intent to preserve competition by preventing undue market concentration, the courts have focused primarily on the likelihood that the consolidation will substantially lessen competition. In this regard, the competitive evil of a horizontal merger is that it places great economic power in the hands of a few businesses, which in turn forecloses business opportunities for smaller firms. Ultimately, however, the primary concern is the impact of the merger on market conditions. Thus, the market share controlled by a merged firm is a critical factor, as is the degree of concentration in the market.

Even if the surviving merged company would possess a nondominant share of the market, the merger may be enjoined. For example, one merger that would have resulted in 30 percent control of the commercial banking market was enjoined[232]; another that would have resulted in 25 percent control of the metal and glass container industries also was prohibited.[233]

If there are few barriers to market entry, mergers that result in large market shares may have little or no anticompetitive effect. On the other hand, in a concentrated industry or in an industry in which there are regulatory barriers to entry (e.g., the hospital industry), even a small increase in market share through merger is more likely to be challenged. Trends toward market concentration in the industry are also considered. Thus, even if the market would remain competitive after a merger, courts will invalidate the merger if it appears to be one of a series of events that will lead to concentration in the industry over time.[234]

The DOJ also focuses on post-merger market concentration and/or market shares in its *1992 Merger Guidelines*. To calculate market concentration, the DOJ uses the Herfindahl-Hirschman Index (HHI), which is the sum of the square of each firm's market share in the relevant market. Using the HHI, the DOJ developed the following general guidelines:

- If the post-merger HHI is below 1,000, the merger is unlikely to be challenged.
- If the post-merger HHI is between 1,000 and 1,800, the merger is unlikely to be challenged if the HHI increased less than 100 points. Increases of greater than 100 points are more likely to be challenged, depending upon other factors.
- If the post-merger HHI is above 1,800, the merger is likely to be challenged if the HHI increased 100 points or more. If the HHI increases between 50 and 100 points, whether the DOJ will challenge the merger will depend upon other factors. If the HHI increases less than 50 points as the result of a merger, it is less likely to be challenged.[235]

Thus, many acquisitions will pass scrutiny under the HHI guidelines. If a hospital with a 35 percent market share acquires a competitor with a 1 percent share, however, the HHI will increase by more than 50; if the acquired company has a 2 percent share, the HHI will increase by more than 100. Other factors considered under the *1992 Merger Guidelines* are the nature of the product, the terms of the sale, the ease of entry into the market, and the availability of information on transactions in the market.

Hospital Mergers

Mergers and acquisitions among hospitals have become an increasingly frequent and important tool used to cope with increasing health care costs, declining inpatient census, and growing financial pressures on hospitals. Over the past decade, there has been a dramatic increase in hospitals deciding to cut costs, increase quality, and improve access to care by merging, affiliating, integrating, and consolidating themselves. Not surprisingly, this trend has led to increased scrutiny by the antitrust enforcement agencies.

During the 1980s, the number of government actions against hospital mergers averaged one per year, but in the 1990s that number has skyrocketed to a current estimate of approximately one action per month brought by either the federal government or state governments.[236] Many of these cases, however, have been closed after an investigation resulting in a finding that the hospital merger or acquisition raised no potential antitrust concerns.

The agencies' first enforcement actions in this area, initiated for the most part during the mid to late 1980s and early 1990s, were generally successful prosecutions settled by consent decree between the government and for-profit health care systems seeking to acquire hospital corporations. In *Hospital Corp. of America,*[237] for example, a for-profit health care corporation entered into a consent decree with the FTC upon the agency's determination that the corporation had violated Section 7 of the Clayton Act in purchasing two other hospital corporations; under the terms of that decree, the defendant health care system agreed to divest two of the hospitals for which it had acquired ownership. The FTC found that the acquisitions increased market concentration substantially in the already concentrated market for general acute care hospital services in an urban area of Chattanooga, Tennessee. The FTC also relied on evidence of significant barriers to entry posed by applicable CON laws and regulations.

Similarly, in a more recent case, the FTC challenged a for-profit health care corporation's acquisition of three hospitals in the three-county area around Salt Lake City, Utah; the corporation already operated two small hospitals in the area.[238] The corporation entered into a consent decree that permitted the acquisition on condition that it divest one of the three acquired hospitals within six months. There have been several other cases involving for-profit health care systems wherein the government has issued a consent decree either enjoining the proposed merger or acquisition, ordering divestiture of an acquired entity, or allowing an acquisition to proceed, but only under specified terms.[239]

In recent years, however, the federal enforcement agencies have not been as successful in resolving challenged merger transactions via consent decree. For example, when two cases involving merger transactions between for-profit hospital entities came before federal courts in 1995, neither resulted in a judgment in favor of the agencies. These two challenges—one brought by the FTC and the other by the DOJ—were rejected on the basis of the agencies' arguments concerning relevant market definition. In both cases, the courts indicated that the government's failure to consider the fluid, dynamic nature of geographic health care markets played a large role in its defeat.

In the FTC action *Federal Trade Commission v. Freeman Hospital,*[240] the Eighth Circuit held that the FTC was not entitled to a preliminary injunction to bar further consolidation of the second and third largest of three acute care hospitals located in Joplin, Missouri. In affirming the lower court's decision, the court upheld a ruling that the relevant geographic market for examining the competitive effects of the merger was not the 27-mile radius around Joplin, as alleged by the FTC and supported by hospital admissions records evidencing current hospital usage. The court agreed with the lower court's determination that the more appropriate geographic market definition takes account of where consumers could practically turn for alternative acute care services, and includes 17 hospitals located up to 54 miles from Joplin.

Similarly, in *United States v. Mercy Health Services,*[241] a federal district court in Iowa denied a request from the DOJ to enjoin the merger of the only two acute care hospitals in Dubuque, Iowa. Rejecting the government's reliance on a narrow geographic market, the court sharply criticized the government for failing to understand the emerging health care market. For example, the court explained, the government erroneously contended that there is strong physician-patient loyalty, which would imply a lack of willingness to change providers; in reality, patients readily switch providers in response to financial incentives or employers' choice of health plan. Another major error, according to the court, was the government's assertion that outreach clinics have little effect on hospitalization patterns. To the contrary, relevant markets can no longer be defined according to the proximity of patients to a particular hospital if there are outreach clinics that facilitate referrals to hospitals some distance away, the court concluded.

Despite the agencies' defeat in some recent hospital merger cases, hospitals engaged in mergers and acquisitions or other consolidations should remain concerned about whether their transactions will withstand the scrutiny of an antitrust investigation by the federal agencies or state government authorities. The following sections address four types of hospital mergers that are potentially permissible in light of recent developments in this area: (1) hospital mergers falling within the agencies' safety zone for such mergers; (2) state-regulated combinations (e.g., mergers subject to state regulation, often pursuant to consent decree between the state and the merging entities); (3) partial combinations (e.g., merger-like transactions that more closely resemble joint ventures to provide certain services); and (4) mergers between nonprofit hospitals.

Safety Zone for Hospital Mergers

Mergers fitting within the "safety zone" for hospital mergers, as outlined in Statement 1 of the agencies' *1996 Policy Statements,*[242] are not likely to be challenged absent extraordinary circumstances. Statement 1 creates a safety zone for mergers where one of the merging hospitals is small. The agencies will not likely challenge a merger between two general acute care hospitals where one of the merging hospitals has fewer than 100 licensed beds, has an average daily inpatient census of fewer than 40 patients, and is more than five years old.

Most hospital mergers will not qualify for the safety zone. For transactions outside the safety zone, the statements offer little guidance, other than listing reasons why the agencies have declined to challenge particular hospital mergers in the past. Such situations include transactions where the agencies found that:

- the merger would not increase the likelihood of the exercise of market power either because of the existence post-merger of strong competitors or because the merging hospitals were sufficiently differentiated
- the merger would allow the hospitals to realize significant cost savings that could not otherwise be realized
- the merger would eliminate a hospital that likely would fail if it continued to operate independently

The agencies also have indicated that, with respect to analyzing hospital mergers that fall outside the safety zone, they will follow the five-step analysis set forth in the *1992 Merger Guidelines*. The five-step process involves an assessment of whether:

1. the merger will significantly increase concentration and result in a concentrated market
2. the transaction raises concerns about potential anticompetitive effects
3. the market entry would be timely and sufficient to defeat anticompetitive effects
4. the efficiency gains can be reasonably achieved by other means
5. whether "but for" the merger either party would fail, thereby causing their assets to leave the relevant market[243]

Although it is debatable whether the agencies intended to relax the requirements for approval of hospital mergers falling within the safety zone, the merger guidelines appear to contain more stringent requirements for approval of a merger based on cost savings or failing company than are implied in the new policy statement. For example, items that do not appear in the new policy statement but do appear in the merger guidelines include a requirement of showing that cost savings will be passed on to consumers to establish an efficiencies defense, or that there is no available less competitive, alternative purchaser of a failing hospital to establish a failing company defense.

State-Regulated Combinations

By entering into a consent decree with a state government, merging parties may find that they are able to bring to a close a potential or parallel federal investigation of a proposed transaction. Although neither the FTC nor the DOJ has announced its official policy concerning their enforcement activity in lieu of state consent decrees, and the possibility always exists that the federal government will challenge a merger without regard to action taken by a state, no proposed hospital merger settled by a state consent decree has been challenged by the federal government. In addition, the DOJ has recently deferred to a state hospital merger investigation, as discussed next. Thus, it appears that involvement by a state's attorney general may eliminate or reduce the scope of a federal investigation.

A recent hospital merger investigated by the Commonwealth of Pennsylvania and the federal DOJ provides an example of how a federal investigation may be unnecessary after a state consent decree.[244] In 1994, the state attorney general's office and the federal agency conducted an investigation of the proposed merger of two hospital systems, and subsequently filed a complaint alleging that the proposed merger would result in high market concentration for inpatient acute care hospital services in the relevant geographic market. More specifically, the proposed merger would combine the only two hospitals in the city of Williamsport, Pennsylvania, and three of the four hospitals in the nearby county. The merger was allowed to proceed, but only under the highly regulatory terms of a settlement agreement between the state and the hospitals. Subsequent to the entry of the consent decree, which is effective for 10 years, the DOJ closed its investigation without taking further action.

The consent decree imposes many requirements on the merging hospitals, including:

- caps on net inpatient revenue per admission, with excess to be reimbursed to payers in subsequent years
- a prohibition on tying between hospital services and DME, nonemergency transport, or home health services
- delicensure of at least 148 beds by the post-merger hospital system
- no expansion of tertiary services for five years
- submission of an annual report to the state attorney general, and payment to that office for cost analysis

The decree also contains restrictions designed to ensure that, post-merger, the hospitals' claimed efficiencies will be passed on to consumers, including a provision requiring the resulting hospital system to achieve certain minimum cost savings within five years, 80 percent of which will be passed on to consumers according to a specified schedule.

The consent decree also regulates the hospital system's relations with third-party payers, as well as with physicians. Thus, although state-regulated mergers may avoid lengthy antitrust litigation, merging hospitals should keep in mind that a state-issued consent decree may subject the post-merger entity to strict regulatory oversight for the first decade of its existence.

Partial Combinations

Another route for avoiding prolonged litigation of a hospital merger may be for the hospitals to combine only partially through the formation of a joint venture, thus abandoning a merger transaction. In one recent case, for example, two of the largest hospitals in Pinella County, Florida, were prohibited from completing their proposed merger but allowed to form a joint venture to deliver most of their services.[245] The hospitals' proposed merger was challenged by Florida's attorney general and the DOJ, which jointly filed suit and a request for injunction in federal district court. Following pretrial preparation, however, the federal and state governments reached a settlement with the hospitals under which the hospitals agreed to forgo their proposed merger and form a joint venture that allowed for consolidation in only service areas that would result in few, if any, adverse effects on competition.

The consent judgment provides that the hospitals may create a new entity organized as a partnership to control their outpatient, administrative, high-tech medical, and most ancillary operations. The hospitals also are allowed to share medical staff. The hospitals must, however, continue the independent provision of general inpatient acute care hospital services, as well as obstetrics, pediatrics, and emergency department operations. In addition, the hospitals must price, market, and sell their services, including those obtained from the joint venture, in active competition with each other. To achieve continued rivalry between the hospitals, the consent judgment mandates procedures for ensuring that individuals or entities affiliated with one hospital do not share competitively sensitive information (i.e., information concerning pricing, managed care contracts, marketing, or planning) with persons affiliated with the other hospital. The judgment also calls for ongoing court jurisdiction, both to monitor compliance and to allow the hospitals to add services for inclusion in the joint venture with the permission of the government.

Merging hospitals should consider whether a partial merger such as the one arrived at under the *Mortan Plant/Mease* settlement meets their objectives, and, if not, the reasons that a complete merger is necessary. A number of factors will affect whether this type of joint venture will meet the hospitals' objectives, including the extent of competition for services to be provided by the joint venture, the existence of duplicative services that could be eliminated through consolidation, and the strength of the antitrust challenge against a full merger.

Mergers Involving Nonprofit Hospitals

Courts have widely accepted that for-profit hospital mergers are horizontal mergers subject to Section 7 of the Clayton Act; the issue of whether that same section applies to nonprofit hospitals has not been settled, however. The DOJ's antitrust charges against two proposed nonprofit hospital mergers have resulted in two very different outcomes. In *United States v. Rockford Memorial Corp.*,[246] the Seventh Circuit affirmed a lower court's judgment that a merger transaction involving two nonprofit hospitals violated both Section 7 of the Clayton Act and the Sherman Act. The case involved the proposed merger of two nonprofit, nonstock, acute care hospitals. In determining whether the merger was subject to Section 7 of the Clayton Act, the court held that the manner of acquiring ownership is not as important as whether the new corporation acquires the economic power of the prior entities. It found that Section 7 applied in this case because the merger would produce a new entity with continuity of management and personnel, plus combined economic power.[247] Analyzing market power under a definition of relevant product market as acute inpatient hospital services (exclusive of outpatient services), the court highlighted evidence indicating that if the merger were approved, the hospitals would control 90 percent of the inpatient hospital business in the area. The court further determined that there were significant barriers to the entry of new competitors and ultimately concluded that the hospitals had not shown that there would be a net economic benefit for consumers or that the merger would be likely to substantially lessen competition.

The court therefore prohibited the hospitals from carrying out the proposed merger.

The Fourth Circuit, on the other hand, in *United States v. Carilion Health System*[248] affirmed a lower court's decision that Section 7 of the Clayton Act does not apply to mergers of nonprofit entities. The case involved one nonstock, nonprofit hospital that owned several nonprofit and for-profit facilities, and another nonstock, nonprofit hospital. The lower court concluded that the merger was exempt from Section 7 because the law does not apply to nonstock acquisitions but rather applies to asset acquisitions by persons subject to FTC jurisdiction. The FTC does not have jurisdiction over nonprofit entities, such as the hospitals in this case, the court explained. Turning to analysis of the alleged Sherman Act violations, the court found the product market to be broader than acute inpatient hospital services because hospitals also compete with outpatient providers. Ultimately, it concluded that the merger would not constitute an unreasonable restraint of trade because the competition in the area outweighed the increased market share the merged facilities would obtain.

The federal antitrust enforcement agencies have consistently taken the position that nonprofit status is not a valid defense to charges that a hospital merger violates antitrust law,[249] at least one recent court decision, *FTC v. Butterworth Health Corp.*, indicates that merging nonprofit hospitals should consider such status as a potential additional defense.[250] In challenging the merger of two large nonprofit hospitals that together provide most of the acute care inpatient services in Grand Rapids, Michigan, the FTC successfully established its prima facie case under Section 7 of the Clayton Act based on statistical evidence that the proposed merger would result in an entity controlling an undue percentage share of the relevant market, and in a significant increase in market concentration. Nonetheless, the federal district court denied the FTC's motion for a preliminary injunction to prevent consummation of the merger. The court reasoned that the merged entity was unlikely to exercise its market power in a way that would hurt consumers chiefly because of its nonprofit status, community board representation, and a stated commitment to constrain prices. Evidence of the hospitals' nonprofit status and the loyalty of board members to community interests suggested that a "substantial increase in market concentration among [the] hospitals is not likely to result in price increases," according to the court.

The court also acknowledged the traditional rule that nonprofit enterprises are not exempt from the antitrust laws, but noted that courts have "implied openness to considering nonprofit status as a relevant consideration if supported by other evidence that anticompetitive effects would not be produced." In highlighting such evidence, the court referred to the cost savings claimed by the defendant-hospitals, such as savings derived from avoiding capital expenditures and achieving operating efficiencies through coordination of activities and elimination of duplicative services. Under these circumstances, the merger is in the public's best interest, the court held, but as a condition of ruling in favor of the hospitals, ordered them to sign and submit for approval a proposed consent decree incorporating a formal "community commitment" plan reiterating the hospitals' intent that cost savings be passed on to consumers. A federal appeals court subsequently affirmed the lower court's decision, finding that the court had carefully weighed the evidence in deciding that the public interest would best be served by allowing the hospitals to proceed with the merger.

Vertical Consolidations

Consolidation between a supplier and a customer (i.e., a vertical consolidation) upsets the normal market forces of supply and demand. Either the supplier or the customer is removed from a segment of the market, which deprives its rivals of an opportunity to compete for that company's business. The size of the market foreclosed in this manner must be substantial before the vertical consolidation becomes unlawful. The test of legality involves an examination of various economic factors to determine if the arrangement is the type that the antitrust laws are intended to proscribe.

In analyzing the competitive effect of vertical mergers, the courts have focused their examination primarily on the following seven factors:

1. market share foreclosed to competitors
2. nature and purpose of the vertical arrangement
3. actual and probable effects on local industry and small businesses
4. level and trend of concentration in the market and the market shares of the participating companies
5. trend toward vertical integration and consolidation in the industry
6. barriers to entry
7. economies of scale[251]

Whether a particular vertical consolidation is permissible depends in part on the degree of market foreclosure; however, this is not the sole factor. The anticompetitive effect that makes a vertical consolidation unlawful also may be found when a competitor is forced out of business as a result of the merger.[252]

Conglomerate Consolidations

Mergers and acquisitions in which there is no apparent relationship between the acquiring and the acquired firm are called conglomerate mergers. These mergers are a result of diversification and do not involve the relationships found in either horizontal or vertical mergers. For example, if AT&T acquired a proprietary hospital chain, the merger would be characterized as a conglomerate. Although it is perhaps less certain, a hospital's acquisition of a nursing home or home health agency may also be characterized as a conglomerate merger.

Conglomerate mergers have several potentially anticompetitive effects. Not only do they combine vast financial resources, thereby placing smaller competitors at a severe disadvantage, but also they may increase barriers to entry in the market. Conglomerate mergers have been condemned when they eliminate a "potential entrant." Firms inside oligopolistic markets perceive certain firms outside the market as potential entrants and therefore depress prices and profit margins to deter entry by these firms either through a new operation or through a toehold acquisition of a small existing firm in the market. If a perceived potential entrant enters the market through the acquisition of a large existing firm, it no longer poses a competitive threat to those already in the market.[253]

For example, a hospital with the largest market share in a particular geographical area may be perceived as a potential entrant into the nursing home market. Its mere presence, "waiting in the wings," has a procompetitive effect on the market because it discourages nursing homes from seeking monopoly profits. In addition, the hospital may exercise a procompetitive effect by acquiring a single nursing home or other less effective competitor. If it acquired the dominant nursing home competitor, however, the market would be stabilized, and any potential procompetitive impact that the hospital could exercise in the nursing home market would be lost.

Under the *1992 Merger Guidelines*, conglomerate mergers are treated the same as vertical mergers.[254] Thus, only mergers in concentrated markets are likely to be challenged.

Pre-Merger Notification Process

Section 7A of the Clayton Act, popularly known as the Hart-Scott-Rodino (HSR) Antitrust Improvements Act of 1976,[255] requires premerger notification of the FTC and the DOJ if a health care organization to be acquired has total assets of $10 million or more and the acquiring company has total assets or annual net sales of $100 million or more, or if the acquired organization has annual net sales or total assets of $100 million or more and the acquiring company has total assets or annual net sales of $10 million or more. Essentially the same rules apply to acquisitions in which the health care organization is the acquirer.[256] Pre-merger notification is required in these instances if, as a result of the acquisition, the acquiring health care organization would hold 15 percent or more of the voting securities or assets of the acquired company, or if it would hold an aggregate total amount of the voting securities and assets in excess of $15 million. The acquiring entity must pay a filing fee of $45,000.

Thus, the pre-merger notification requirement applies only to comparatively large acquisitions. In such transactions, the entities involved should never assume that failure to file may result in the agencies' overlooking the merger or acquisition; most sizable transactions come to the government's attention even where a filing does not occur. Federal antitrust investigators read through health care publications, receive information about transactions from state regulatory agencies, and also receive complaints from third-party payers and other private entities affected by a proposed transaction.

When the Hart-Scott-Rodino filing requirements apply to a transaction, the merger or acquisition may not be consummated until after the expiration of a 30-day waiting period from the date of filing (15 days in the case of a tender offer). The antitrust agency must decide within the 30-day period whether the transaction requires a "second request" for further information. A second request usually seeks all documents created by the parties about the transaction and competition issues. In the health care context, this includes documents about competitors, relations with managed care organizations, financial issues, and efficiencies. The scope of the second request can be reduced through negotiations with the agencies.

Merging entities may want to design a plan to avoid a second request when a second request appears possible. A presentation should persuade the agencies that the antitrust issues are clear and a second request is unnecessary, and such a presentation must be made to the agencies before the Hart-Scott-Rodino filing. Second requests do not necessarily result in lengthy investigations. The antitrust agencies sometimes will engage in a "quick look," under which they analyze a critical antitrust issue without the entire second request investigation; if unable to resolve that issue, however, the agencies will likely proceed with the investigation.

The agencies recently revised their pre-merger notification procedures for reviewing mergers by jointly adopting new procedural steps designed to accelerate the review process, lower the cost of compliance, and better coordinate the agencies' investigation of merger activity.[257] These steps include:

- expediting decisions as to which agency will investigate a proposed merger transaction, with a decision made within nine days of receiving HSR Notification and Report Form;
- jointly developing and issuing a uniform model for second requests, which will ensure greater consistency between the agencies;
- arranging joint preclearance meetings, in certain circumstances, for the parties involved to get more information and allow for analysis of proposed transactions even before it has been decided which agency will have jurisdiction;
- jointly adopting a formal appeals process for disputes over second request compliance;
- jointly adopting a new "quick look" approach to merger review, under which the agencies will attempt to narrow their focus to include only the determinative issues, and the parties will be invited to identify issues that they perceive to be most significant;
- conducting joint training and other activities to improve staff investigatory skills;
- proposing new regulations to increase and clarify circumstances under which transactions are exempt from filing requirements.

If the government ultimately decides that the transaction would be unlawful, it has a number of options. It may attempt to enjoin the transaction in court or negotiate a compromise with the merging entities. The elements of a negotiated compromise ("consent decree") will vary; for example, a consent decree may permit the merger but require the transfer of savings to the local community, or permit the merger of only some hospital services. State enforcement officials are much more likely to be open to "regulatory" decrees than are federal antitrust investigators. The government also may decide to take no action, but reserve the right to break up the merged entity in the future.

Defenses

In responding to an antitrust challenge to a proposed transaction, health care organizations may turn to any of several possible defense strategies. Perhaps the most obvious of these defenses is to contradict a plaintiff's allegations concerning the relevant market and dispute evidence of probable competitive effects of a merger or acquisition. A health care organization may also prevail in the face of a merger challenge by asserting an affirmative defense (i.e., a defense that justifies an otherwise illegal transaction), although successful assertion of such a defense requires the defendant-organization to carry the burden of proof. The following sections discuss the two most common of these affirmative defenses: (1) the failing company defense, and (2) the efficiencies defense.

Failing Company Defense

The failing company defense provides a complete defense to an otherwise illegal merger under Section 7 of the Clayton Act, if all elements of the defense are satisfied at the time of the merger. The courts created the failing company defense against antitrust allegations on the theory that the acquisition of a failing company does not lessen competition substantially.[258] This doctrine is narrowly construed, however, and has been applied only if the company probably would have been unable to meet its financial obligations in the near future or to reorganize successfully.[259] In addition, under the *1992 Merger Guidelines*, the failing company must have made unsuccessful good-faith attempts to obtain reasonable alternative offers of acquisition before the defense will apply.[260]

A variation of this defense was applied in *Oleksy v. Sisters of Mercy*.[261] In that case, the hospital required a capital input of several million dollars to meet state standards. The Sisters of Mercy decided that they would be unable to assume a debt of this size and offered the hospital for sale. Even though the purchaser was the hospital's primary competitor, the acquisition was approved because no other purchaser reasonably could be found.

Efficiency/Procompetitive Effects

A defense based on the efficiency/procompetitive effects of a merger has been judicially created in accordance with the legislative history of the 1950 amendments to the Clayton Act; some supporters of these amendments noted that competition may be enhanced as a result of certain mergers.[262] Although the defense has rarely been invoked successfully, the Supreme Court, in dictum, has recognized possible procompetitive effects when two smaller firms merge to improve their ability to compete with a large, dominant competitor.[263]

In its *1992 Merger Guidelines*, the DOJ indicated that the presence of efficiencies may grow in significance as a factor in merger analysis, and it recognized that a merger's primary benefit is its potential for enhancing efficiency.[264] The agency stated that even when it would otherwise challenge a merger, it might refrain from such a challenge if the merging parties meet their burden of proof in showing that the merger would produce substantial cost savings through economies of scale, integration of production facilities, plant specialization, lower transportation costs, or other efficiencies in specific business activities. In addition, the DOJ indicated that it might take into account under certain circumstances reductions in general selling, administrative, and overhead expenses. Thus, it is possible that certain health care acquisitions could be justified on the grounds of efficiency. However, the DOJ has also stated that it will reject efficiency claims if equivalent results are achievable by other means.

In 1997, the DOJ and the FTC announced the revision of a portion of their joint *1992 Merger Guidelines* to clarify how the agencies analyze merging entities' claims that the merger will achieve efficiencies, such as lower costs or improved product quality, that should be taken into account in assessing the merger's competitive effects.[265] The revisions affect Section 4 of the *1992 Merger Guidelines*, which relates to efficiency justifications that may be asserted for a merger, and are intended to provide the public, enforcement agencies, courts, and merging entities with a better understanding of how claimed efficiencies will be evaluated, and whether such efficiencies will make a difference in the agencies' analysis of a proposed merger.

Among other clarifications, the revisions:

- Explain how efficiencies may affect the analysis of whether a proposed merger may likely result in significant lessening of competition in a relevant market.
- Define more precisely how the agencies determine if claimed efficiencies are properly attributable to the proposed merger.
- Clarify what merging entities must do to substantiate their efficiencies claims.
- Outline the circumstances, as a practical matter, in which the agencies are likely to find efficiencies claims persuasive.

Although acknowledging that mergers can result in efficiencies that will enhance the merged entities' ability to compete by lowering prices, creating new products, or improving quality of existing products or services, the revised Section 4 cautions that such efficiencies will not necessarily prevent the agencies from condemning an otherwise anticompetitive merger.

JOINT VENTURES AND PROVIDER NETWORKS

The difference between a merger and a joint venture is that the parties in a merger integrate their operations completely, while the parties in a joint venture remain independent and integrate their operations only partially and only for the purposes of a particular venture. There are a wide variety of joint ventures in the health care field, including horizontal joint ventures between physicians and/or hospitals, and vertical and conglomerate joint ventures between physicians/hospitals and, for example, DME companies or home health entities to provide DME or home health services, respectively. In addition, hospitals may undertake joint ventures with each other or with medical professionals to establish satellite facilities or to form HMOs, PPOs, or other types of health care delivery systems.

Joint Ventures To Provide Services or Products

Joint ventures pose unique problems in antitrust analysis because they have characteristics of agreements covered by the Sherman Act and characteristics of mergers covered by the Clayton Act. Viewed in the abstract, the very creation of the venture could be characterized as an agreement by the venturers not to compete. In addition, the operational agreements of the joint venture could raise issues such as price fixing, particularly if the parents contract with the joint venture entity. Because the joint venture company is itself a new competitor in the market, however, its competitive impact must be considered in evaluating the legality of the venture.

Antitrust Analysis

The initial factor that must be considered in determining the legality of a joint venture is its purpose. Clearly, if the joint venture is undertaken to accomplish a goal otherwise prohibited by the antitrust laws (e.g., price fixing or market allocation), courts will view the activities of the joint venture entity as the concerted actions of its parents rather than as the action of a unitary entity.

If the joint venture enables the parents to accomplish a legitimate objective, however, courts will apply a rule-of-reason analysis, looking to the joint venture's competitive effect to determine its legality under the Clayton Act. This analysis focuses on:

- the relationship between the parents and the joint venture market
- the parents' possession of a large market share in their own markets and substantial size in relation to competitors in the joint venture market
- the inferences of collaboration to be drawn from the nature of the joint venture
- the possibility of stifling the competitive potential of the joint venture
- the possible "spill-over" collusion between the parents

- the probability that, in the absence of the joint venture, the parents would either enter the market independently or exercise a procompetitive influence on the market as potential competition[266]

Because the venturers are unlikely to compete with their progeny in the future, the court evaluating the anticompetitive effect of a joint venture not only must evaluate the circumstances existing at the time the joint venture was undertaken, but also must predict the venturers' probable future courses of conduct. If both parents would have entered the market independently, the joint venture clearly has some anticompetitive effect. Nevertheless, a question would remain as to whether the effect "may be to substantially lessen competition." If only one parent would have entered the market, the analysis is somewhat less clear. A joint venture will probably be found illegal, however, if (1) the in-the-market parent has a monopoly or dominant market position; (2) the other parent is a substantial, clearly recognized potential entrant; and (3) there are no other, or very few other, potential entrants.[267]

The market power of the joint venture entity must also be considered in evaluating the permissibility of a joint venture. Like a merger, a joint venture that results in a large aggregation of market power may be prohibited under the antitrust laws. A joint venture between a hospital and a company to provide DME, for example, was determined to be in violation of antitrust laws where the hospital had market power, with almost 80 percent of the hospital services market.[268] Of crucial importance to the plaintiff-DME company's case was evidence indicating that the DME market share of the hospital-company increased from 9 percent to 60 percent in a few years while the market share of the plaintiff declined from 73 percent to 30 percent. A jury awarded the competitor damages that were trebled to more than $2 million. A district court then ruled in favor of the hospital, but the Eleventh Circuit reversed and reinstated the jury verdict.

In contrast, a federal district court ruled against a supplier of DME that alleged various violations of federal antitrust law arising from the joint venture between a hospital and a competing DME company where the joint venture's market share peaked at 44 percent, averaged 33 percent, and at the end of its six-year existence, was steadily losing market share to other DME suppliers.[269] The federal district court ruled in favor of the joint venture partners, finding that the competing DME supplier had failed to come forward with sufficient evidence of the alleged antitrust violations. There was no showing of unreasonable restraint of trade; in fact, after entry of the joint venture into the market, there was neither an appreciable rise in price or reduction in quality of DME, nor a decrease in the number of firms supplying DME in the hospital's service area.

Safety Zones for Certain Hospital Joint Ventures

The DOJ and the FTC have taken the position that most hospital joint ventures to purchase, operate, and market the services of high technology or other expensive medical equipment do not create antitrust problems.[270] The agencies have created a safety zone for these activities (as outlined in Statement 2 of the agencies' *1996 Policy Statements*), and absent extraordinary circumstances, will not challenge such a joint venture if the venture includes only the number of hospitals whose participation is needed to support the equipment. A joint venture that includes other hospitals will not be challenged if the additional hospitals would not be able to support the equipment on their own or through the formation of a competing joint venture.

If such a joint venture falls outside the safety zone, it does not necessarily raise significant antitrust concern, and will be analyzed under the rule of reason. Assuming that the joint venture is permissible and that the joint activities can be characterized as those of a unitary entity, the antitrust implications of agreements between the joint venture entity and its parents must be examined. If such agreements are ancillary to the operation of the joint venture, they are analyzed under the rule of reason. If such agreements merely further the interests of the parents, however, the joint venture entity may be characterized as a subterfuge, and the per se standard may be applied.

Statement 3 in the agencies' *1996 Policy Statements* applies to joint ventures between hospitals to provide specialized, expensive services that require investments that a single hospital might be unable to justify (e.g., services that require the recruitment and training of specialized personnel would fall under this statement).[271] In this statement, the agencies declare that most of these types of joint ventures do not create antitrust problems. The statement does not create a safety zone, however, because the agencies' have declined to do so on the basis of their need to acquire more expertise in evaluating the cost of, demand for, and potential benefits from such joint ventures before they can articulate a meaningful safety zone. Instead, the statement provides that the agencies will apply a rule of reason analysis to a specialized clinical integrated joint venture as long as the venture is not merely a pretext for restricting competition.

Within the statement, the agencies also provide an example to provide additional guidance in this area. The facts of the example involve two general acute care hospitals (located in a town with a population of approximately 75,000) that seek to enter into a joint venture to provide open-heart surgery. Neither hospital currently provides open-heart surgery or has plans to do so on its own, and the town does not have sufficient demand to support more than one local open-heart facility. The joint venture has made plans to protect against exchanges of competitive information. Under these circumstances, the agencies state that they would not challenge the joint venture because it does not eliminate any existing or potential competition and because it does not include collateral agreements or conditions that might restrict competition.

In discussing collateral agreements to a venture, the agencies further provide an example in which the facts involve the formation of a joint venture to provide highly sophisticated oncology services, and the participants of the venture also agree on the prices to charge for all radiology services, regardless of whether the services are provided to patients undergoing oncology radiation therapy. Under these circumstances, the agencies would view the joint venture as legal, but the collateral agreement as unrelated to achieving the purpose of the joint venture and therefore illegal price fixing.

Joint Purchasing Arrangements

The DOJ and the FTC have created a safety zone for joint purchasing arrangements among health care providers.[272] In Statement 7, the agencies recognize that most joint purchasing arrangements among hospitals or other health care providers allow the participants to achieve efficiencies that will benefit consumers, and do not raise antitrust concerns. Under the safety zone, the agencies will not challenge joint purchasing arrangements among health care providers when (1) the purchases account for less than 35 percent of the total sales of the purchased product or service in the relevant market, and (2) the cost of the products and services purchased jointly accounts for less than 20 percent of the total revenues from all products or services sold by each competing participant in the joint purchasing arrangement.

The purpose of the first condition is to ascertain if the arrangement might drive down below competitive levels the price of the product or service being purchased. The second condition pertains to the possibility that a joint purchasing arrangement might result in standardized costs, thereby facilitating price fixing or otherwise having anticompetitive effects. This condition applies when only some or all of the participants are direct competitors.

The agencies also provide guidance for joint purchasing arrangements that fall outside the antitrust safety zone. The policy statement indicates that there are several safeguards that joint purchasing arrangements can adopt to mitigate antitrust concerns. First, antitrust concerns are lessened if members are not required to use the arrangement for all their purchases of a particular product or service. Members can be asked to commit to purchase a voluntarily specified amount so that a volume discount or other favorable contract can be negotiated. Second, antitrust risk is lowered when negotiations are conducted on behalf of the joint purchasing arrangement by an independent employee or agent who is not also an employee of a participant. Third, when communications between the purchasing group and each individual participant are kept confidential, and not discussed with or disseminated to other participants, the likelihood of anticompetitive communications is lessened.

Because there are a large number and variety of purchasing groups in the health care field, the agencies conclude that there are no significant entry barriers to forming new groups. Therefore, it is not necessary to open a joint purchasing arrangement to all competitors in the market. Exclusion of some competitors will raise antitrust concerns only if those excluded are put at a significant competitive disadvantage in competing with the participants.

Joint Ventures with HMOs and Other Prepaid Plans

Hospitals may enter into joint ventures with other health care institutions and professionals to form an HMO or other prepaid plan. The antitrust implications of such a joint venture, which are largely dependent on the extent of provider control, were discussed at length in a policy statement issued by the FTC in 1981.[273] In general, the FTC believes that HMOs and other prepaid plans have significant potential both to promote competition in the health care marketplace and to restrain competition because they usually involve a combination of physicians and institutions. As a result of their procompetitive potential, however, the FTC has stated that the activities of prepaid health plans should be governed by the rule of reason and should not be declared per se illegal.

The FTC distinguishes between nonprovider-controlled plans and provider-controlled plans. Nonprovider-controlled plans are treated as single entities, raising antitrust concerns only when they (1) take concerted action with third parties, (2) attempt to monopolize, or (3) exercise monopoly power. In contrast, actions taken by provider-controlled plans are viewed as concerted activity subject to the antitrust laws. As a result, a provider-controlled plan may be found to violate the antitrust laws by merely establishing plan policies.

Control is viewed as a question of fact to be determined on a case-by-case basis. Provider control is most easily demonstrated when the provider organization owns the plan or selects a majority of the voting members of the plan's governing body. Although a provider organization selects only a minority of the governing body members, it may be found to control the plan if that minority has the practical ability to make policy. The FTC has indicated, however, that it is unlikely to find control when a provider organization selects fewer than one-fourth of the governing body members and there is no evidence of their dominance over the plan's decision-making process.

Even without organizational control, providers may have practical control of the plan. The FTC has identified the following factors as indicative of control:

- power to vote on plan reimbursement or coverage proposals
- representation on (or selection of) key plan policy-making committees
- delegated authority, including veto or approval power over plan policies
- power to appoint or approve plan management
- financing of plan operations
- interlocking directors, officers, or executives
- absence of other strong interest groups on the governing body

According to the FTC, a provider organization will be found to control a plan when, on the basis of these factors, it has the ability to set overall plan policies.

The FTC's analytical framework for a provider-controlled plan is dependent on the organizational structure of the plan (i.e., whether the plan is a merged plan or a partially integrated plan). In merged plans, functions are totally integrated. In partially integrated plans, the providers continue to compete outside the plan, but integrate some of their practice into the plan or make substantial financial contributions to it. Ordinarily, group and staff model HMOs are considered merged plans, while most individual practice type HMOs are considered partially integrated plans.

Merged plans are analyzed under a traditional merger analysis. Thus, in the absence of an anticompetitive purpose, the formation of such a plan is unlikely to raise antitrust concerns unless 30 percent of the area physicians are involved. Once operational, a merged plan is treated as a single business entity, raising antitrust concerns only in connection with combinations with third parties, attempts to monopolize, or the exercise of monopoly power.

Provided that the plan has no anticompetitive purpose, the FTC will not ordinarily initiate action to prevent the formation of a partially integrated plan, unless the physicians participating in the plan comprise two-thirds or more of the total number of physicians of any significant medical specialty in the area. Participation by a large percentage of area hospitals may raise similar concerns, especially if these participating hospitals are precluded from participating in other plans.

After a partially integrated plan becomes operational, agreements by its controlling providers are analyzed by the FTC under the rule of reason (i.e., only agreements that have significant anticompetitive effects without sufficient counterbalancing procompetitive effects violate the antitrust laws). Plans with no market power, therefore, are not usually challenged by the FTC unless it appears that their policies or practices were developed for an anticompetitive purpose.

On the other hand, if a provider-controlled, partially integrated plan exercises significant market power, it may be challenged on the ground that its policies and practices unreasonably limit competition among participating physicians or unreasonably affect competing providers or plans. The FTC has identified some specific situations in which it believes such antitrust concerns would arise:

- adoption of a reimbursement mechanism that tends to increase physician fees above market levels, thereby reducing existing market incentives for price competition

- unreasonable exclusion of competing providers, when such exclusion results in serious disadvantages for the other providers
- prohibition against participation of plan providers in any other prepaid plan, which, because of the number of participating providers, makes it difficult for other plans to recruit a sufficient panel

Preferred Provider Organizations

Unlike HMOs, PPOs do not perform any insurance function. Moreover, in most PPOs, the providers themselves do not assume any risk, as they are reimbursed on a fee-for-service basis. In evaluating the antitrust risk associated with the operation of a PPO, it is necessary to distinguish between provider-controlled PPOs and payer-controlled PPOs.

Provider-Controlled PPOs

Antitrust analysis of the activities of provider-controlled PPOs is similar to that of the activities of provider-controlled HMOs if the providers have a stake in the success of the PPO as a competitive entity. Thus, if the hospitals and physicians forming a PPO have invested risk capital in the venture and have integrated marketing, claims administration, billing, and other functions, the provider-controlled PPO is likely to be characterized as a legitimate joint venture, rather than as a mere subterfuge enabling competing providers to fix prices.[274] In addition, a PPO is likely to be characterized as a legitimate joint venture if provider participation is limited; agreements among the controlling providers with respect to fees for services provided to patients enrolled in the PPO may be characterized as ancillary to the activities of the venture. Similarly, limitations on the number of providers allowed to participate in the PPO may be permissible when the PPO does not possess undue market power.

In one recent case, for example, the Fifth Circuit held that a PPO's decision not to renew a participation agreement with one hospital after signing such an agreement with a nearby competing hospital did not illegally restrain trade.[275] In so holding, the court upheld a grant of summary judgment in favor of the PPO, but rejected the lower court's reasoning that the excluded hospital lacked antitrust standing due to its failure to show antitrust injury from the alleged conduct. Although affirming the disposition of the case in favor of the PPO, the court found that the lower court erred in concluding that the antitrust injury component of standing embodies a showing of injury to competition in the marketplace as well as appropriate injury to the plaintiff. For standing purposes, the court explained, the antitrust injury issue should be viewed from the perspective of the plaintiff's position in the marketplace, rather than from overall marketplace competition. From that perspective, alleged losses suffered by the excluded hospital as a result of not being able to participate in the PPO fall within the bounds of antitrust injury, and sufficiently establish the hospital's standing to sue the PPO on antitrust grounds.

The appeals court determined that the correct approach in this case is to analyze, for summary judgment purposes, the merits of the alleged antitrust claims. Under that framework, the appeals court found in favor of the PPO because the excluded hospital failed to show that harm to competition resulted from its exclusion from the PPO. Finding that evidence presented by the excluded hospital did not show the hospital's inability to compete because of its termination from the PPO, the court highlighted several facts, including the plaintiff-hospital's affiliation with a larger PPO in the area; the absence of any reduction in the number of providers available to consumers; and the availability of the excluded hospital's services through several other managed care networks.

In another case, a federal court found that a hospital system that participated in a PPO did not unlawfully conspire with the insurer to restrain trade or monopolize the market for hospital services because the insurer unilaterally decided which hospitals would participate, and its decision reflected sound business judgment.[276] The fact that the insurer unilaterally chose the hospitals precluded a finding of unlawful conspiracy. Although the insurer limited an excluded hospital's access to PPO patients by charging enrollees a higher co-payment when they received care at an out-of-network hospital, that was not the type of harm to competition the antitrust laws meant to proscribe, the court concluded.

In *Ball Memorial Hospital, Inc. v. Mutual Hospital Insurance, Inc.*,[277] 80 Indiana acute care hospitals failed to stop the implementation of a new PPO offered by Blue Cross and Blue Shield. The hospitals claimed that the Blues' purpose in offering the PPO was to exclude other PPOs from the market, to extract unreasonable discounts from health care providers through coercion, and to extend its own market position. Charging that this conduct violated federal and state antitrust laws, the hospitals asked a federal court to halt the initiation of the new PPO. The Seventh Circuit refused to delay the PPO's implementation, however, finding that Blue Cross/Blue Shield did not possess sufficient market power to warrant antitrust scrutiny of the PPO. Market power results from the ability to cut back the market's total supply and then raise prices due to consumer demand for the product. In this case, the court found that Blue Cross/Blue Shield did not have such power because they furnished a product, health care financing, that other entities can and do supply easily. The market in health care financing is competitive because the customers can readily switch companies, new suppliers can enter the market quickly, and existing suppliers can expand their sales rapidly, the court explained. Rather than finding the proposed PPO to be an antitrust threat, the court determined that blocking the PPO's implementation would have an anticompetitive effect. Without the PPO, the court explained, buyers of health care financing would have fewer options, and competitors would have one fewer entity to compete with.

Significant antitrust implications for providers may arise in regard to negotiations with PPOs. Although no significant antitrust issues are raised when a PPO negotiates and contracts with providers on an individual basis, negotiations with provider groups carry an antitrust risk for the providers. Because the providers do not have a financial stake in the venture, the bargaining process may be viewed simply as an agreement among providers to negotiate collectively. Thus, elements are present for a PPO to run afoul of antitrust problems, particularly insofar as the PPO attempts to affect prices charged by participating providers.

The DOJ and the FTC, in their *1996 Policy Statements,* have indicated that they will not challenge a PPO having the aim of packaging and marketing less costly medical and/or hospital services where a large percentage of hospitals and physicians in any geographic market have not become affiliated only with the PPO and where the development of other PPOs is not deterred.

Payer-Controlled PPOs

PPOs initiated by third-party payers typically are organized by an entity that pays for health care services or represents individuals who are provided such services, such as a corporate employer, insurance company, or union. Policies set by payer-controlled PPOs with respect to participation limits, exclusivity, or other matters concerning providers should be permissible in most cases. The establishment of such policies by a payer-controlled PPO will be viewed as a vertical restraint and will be judged by rule-of-reason standards. If, however, the PPO has substantial market power and employs it to coerce providers into accepting unfavorable and socially undesirable goals, its activities may be held to be unreasonable.[278]

It is also worth noting that agreements between two or more third-party payers with respect to who will be providers do not constitute a naked restraint of trade subject to the per se rule. Joint buying ventures generally are lawful enterprises that perform a procompetitive function through the achievement of economies of scale and other efficiencies. [For a related discussion, see Joint Purchasing Arrangements.]

Provider Networks

Antitrust issues faced by networks of health care providers have received a great deal of attention over the last several years. The antitrust enforcement agencies have issued detailed statements of their enforcement policies with respect to such networks:[279] Statement 8 covers physician network joint ventures, and Statement 9 covers multiprovider networks, which are defined as ventures among providers that jointly market their services to health benefits plans and other purchasers. These two statements describe in detail the agencies' analytical approach when confronted with a network of otherwise independent health care providers who seek to provide their services to a health care plan through a contractual arrangement. Both statements make a critical distinction between networks that are not integrated and those in which "the physicians' integration through the network is likely to produce significant efficiencies that benefit consumers."

Integration Defined

According to these statements, the most straightforward way for a physician network to integrate economically is for the physician members to share substantial financial risk in providing all the services that are jointly priced through the network. The agencies provide five examples of what constitutes sharing of substantial financial risk:

1. *Capitation.* An agreement to provide defined health care services to an enrollee in return for a fixed, predetermined amount (usually a "per member/per month" payment), regardless of the level of services actually required; this payment mechanism shifts the financial risk of paying for those services from the enrollee to the provider.
2. *Provision of services on a percentage of premium basis.* A network that provides services to its participating physicians to a health plan on a percentage of premium basis also assumes the financial risk of providing these services; as with capitation, providers are paid a fixed amount per patient to provide designated health services.
3. *Fee-for-service with a risk withhold.* A network assumes risk if it contracts on a fee-for-service basis but withholds a "substantial amount" from distribution to physician members

based on group performance in meeting the cost-containment goals of the network as a whole.

4. *Establishing targets and financial penalties.* Some networks establish overall cost or utilization targets for the network as a whole; participants are rewarded or penalized depending on group performance in meeting the targets. The agencies recognize that such a structure can constitute assumption of risk.
5. *Global rates.* Global or all-inclusive case rates may involve substantial risk sharing if they cover a complex or extended course of treatment that requires the substantial coordination of care by physicians in different specialties offering a complementary mix of services, for a fixed, predetermined payment, where the costs of that course of treatment for any individual patient can vary greatly due to the individual patient's condition, or the choice, complexity, or length of treatment, or other factors.

Capitation and fee-for-service with a risk withhold were included as examples of substantial risk sharing in the first version of the *Policy Statements* issued in 1993; the other examples, however, were added when the *Policy Statements* were reissued in 1996.

Significantly, the *1996 Policy Statements* also recognize that substantial risk sharing is not the only way in which network providers can integrate. According to the agencies, networks "that do not involve the sharing of substantial financial risk" nonetheless lawfully may set prices at which they sell their services if they "involve sufficient integration to demonstrate that the venture is likely to produce significant efficiencies." Such integration can be evidenced by the network implementing an active and ongoing program to evaluate and modify practice patterns by the network's physician participants and creating a high degree of interdependence and cooperation among the physicians to control costs and ensure quality. Such a program might include utilization review, evaluation of individual and aggregate performance, efforts to modify behavior where necessary, case management, review of hospital stays, and development of practice standards and protocols. The statements also comment favorably on selective recruitment of efficient providers and significant investment of capital, "both monetary and human," in the venture. This integration, without sharing substantial financial risk, is frequently referred to as clinical integration.

The *1996 Policy Statements* provide several new examples to further clarify which types of programs would qualify as substantial clinical integration. Although emphasizing the change from per se treatment to rule-of-reason treatment with respect to joint pricing within networks demonstrating substantial clinical integration, the agencies also have clearly indicated that where participating physicians in such a network do not share significant financial risk, the network does not fall within provider-network safety zones outlined in Statement 8.

Thus, the 1996 revision of the agencies' *Policy Statements* marks a shift in enforcement policy with respect to physician and multiprovider networks. Where the agencies formerly stated providers were allowed to establish networks to negotiate and enter into payer contracts only if the network was financially integrated (e.g., capitated payment scheme), the guidelines now make clear that the government will not automatically reject nonfinancially integrated networks. Rather, in evaluating the legality of a network, the agencies will consider other forms of integration such as quality assurance programs, and other measures that indicate that the providers are working together to provide a better product to the market. The significance of this legal development is that it provides wider leeway for providers to join forces and market their services as a collective unit. It remains to be seen whether this leeway will slow the dramatic increase in health care mergers that has occurred over the past few years, and create a new trend of hospitals and other practices remaining legally separate but consolidating their efforts with other providers through joint venture arrangements, or the formation of other loosely affiliated networks.

Joint Pricing and the Messenger Model

Members of networks that have not integrated in any fashion cannot price jointly without violating the per se rule against price fixing. Such networks are relegated to using the so-called messenger model if they wish to collaborate to negotiate with a health plan on prices. The goal of the messenger model is to ensure that each provider in the network makes independent, noncollusive decisions on prices and other competitive terms. Providers who are sufficiently integrated, on the other hand, may jointly set prices without running afoul of the per se rule; agreements on price and other terms of competition among providers in an integrated network are subject to the rule of reason. Accordingly, unless the formation and operation of such a network may have a substantial anticompetitive effect that is not outweighed by any procompetitive efficiencies, such a venture is lawful under the antitrust laws.

As briefly described previously, perhaps the most significant revision in the *1996 Policy Statements* is the agencies' indication that they will, in certain circumstances, grant rule of reason treatment to nonfinancially, or clinically integrated, networks. Before this revision, the agencies considered provider networks to be per se illegal if they were involved in joint pricing and were not financially integrated through a risk-sharing arrangement. Under the new *Policy Statements,* a network may be analyzed under the rule of reason if it includes substantial clinical integration, results in significant efficiencies to consumers, and engages in joint pricing reasonably necessary to achieve those efficiencies.

The *1996 Policy Statements* include examples and revised language approving the use of a more flexible "messenger model" than was allowed under the previous guidelines, which strictly adhered to a model in which the agent for the network did nothing but send offers from payers to each provider who then independently accepted or rejected; the new guidelines specify that it is permissible for the agent to receive some authority in advance from individual providers to accept contract offers on their behalf.

Physician Network Joint Ventures

Statement 8 delineates a narrow safety zone for physician network joint ventures, and also provides that nonfinancially integrated networks of this type that result in significant efficiencies to consumers, and whose joint pricing agreements are reasonably necessary to achieve those efficiencies, are subject to a rule of reason analysis. In determining whether a physician network joint venture is exclusive or nonexclusive, the agencies will examine the following indicia of nonexclusivity, among others:

- that viable competing networks or plans with adequate provider participation currently exist in the market;
- that providers in the network actually participate in other networks or contract individually with health benefits plans, or that there is other evidence of their willingness and incentive to do so;
- that providers in the network earn substantial revenue outside the network;
- the absence of any indication of significant departicipation from other networks in the market; and
- the absence of any indication of coordination among the providers in the network regarding price or other competitively significant terms of participation in other networks or plans.

Revisions that appeared in the *1996 Policy Statements* include a more complete articulation of factors that should be considered in determining whether a physician network is exclusive, and an additional example indicating that a physician network involved in both risk and nonrisk contracting can engage in joint pricing for both types of contracts if the efficiencies from the risk business carry over into the nonrisk business.

Safety Zone for Exclusive Networks

Exclusive physician network joint ventures that comprise no more than 20 percent of the physicians in any specialty in a geographic market, and those physicians have active hospital staff privileges and share substantial financial risk, will not be challenged by the agencies absent extraordinary circumstances. In relevant markets with fewer than five physicians in a particular specialty, an exclusive venture otherwise qualifying for the safety zone may include one physician from that specialty, on a nonexclusive basis, even though the inclusion may result in a venture consisting of more than 20 percent of the physicians in that specialty.

Safety Zone for Nonexclusive Networks

Nonexclusive physician network joint ventures that comprise no more than 30 percent of the physicians in any specialty in a geographic market, and those physicians have active hospital staff privileges and share substantial financial risk, will not be challenged by the agencies absent extraordinary circumstances. In relevant markets with fewer than five physicians in a particular specialty, a nonexclusive venture otherwise qualifying for the safety zone may include one physician from that specialty, on a nonexclusive basis, even though the inclusion may result in a venture consisting of more than 30 percent of the physicians in that specialty.

A nonexclusive network may limit or condition participating providers' freedom to contract outside the network. The agencies caution, however, that if such provisions significantly restrict the ability or willingness of those physicians to participate in other networks or contract on their own with managed care plans, the network will be considered to be exclusive for purposes of the safety zone.

Multiprovider Networks

Statement 9 applies to multiprovider networks, which are defined by the agencies as "ventures among providers that jointly market their health care services to subscribers at jointly determined prices and agree to controls aimed at containing costs and assuring quality." By definition, multiprovider networks are those that involve providers other than just physicians. The agencies indicate in their *1996 Policy Statements* that physician network joint ventures covered under Statement 8 and multiprovider networks covered under Statement 9 are to be analyzed in a virtually parallel manner. Recognizing that many of the issues that arise with physician networks are similar to those in multiprovider networks, the agencies explain in

Statement 9 that the antitrust analysis for these two types of networks should be very similar.

Unlike Statement 8, however, Statement 9 does not provide any safety zones but rather is a statement of analytical principles. The decision not to provide such a safety zone is based on the agencies' view that they do not have sufficient experience analyzing the continually developing new arrangements that fall under this category of network, and therefore are unable to articulate meaningful safety zones.

Essentially, Statement 9 provides no more than that the agencies will apply the antitrust laws to multiprovider networks in the same manner that they apply them to other types of networks. The agencies indicate that they are most concerned with horizontal agreements among competitors, whether at the hospital level, at the physician level, or in terms of individual services. When such agreements exist, the agencies will analyze them under the rule of reason if sufficient economic integration exists to justify them or if the network has substantial clinical integration that is likely to produce significant efficiencies, and the pricing agreements are reasonably necessary to achieve those efficiencies.

Unlike the former Statement 9 in the 1994 version of the *Policy Statements,* which contained no examples pertaining to multiprovider networks, the new Statement 9 contains four examples intended to provide further guidance as to the agencies' analytical approach to such networks. All of the examples use the PHO as the model, but each raises different concerns:

1. a PHO involving substantial clinical integration that would not raise significant competitive concerns under the rule of reason
2. a PHO providing services on a per-case basis that would be analyzed under the rule of reason
3. a PHO involving substantial financial risk sharing and including all of the physicians in a small rural county that would not raise competitive concerns under the rule of reason

4. a PHO not involving horizontal agreements on price, but utilizing a messenger model, with various permutations of that model

Although these hypothetical examples are useful because they indicate how the agencies will apply antitrust principles to concrete fact situations, health care organizations should remember that the helpfulness of the examples is limited by their context. The examples contained in the statements present relatively uncomplicated situations in which the antitrust issues are relatively clear. Other useful sources for the purpose of predicting the agencies' response to the formation of PHOs are recent consent decrees entered between PHOs and the DOJ, although these also are essentially limited to the facts of each case. [For a more detailed discussion of these consent decrees, see Physician Hospital Organizations.]

For a multiprovider network that merits a rule of reason analysis, the agencies will examine the overall competitive effects of the arrangement in the relevant market, balancing the anticompetitive effects against the potential efficiencies. Statement 9 addresses in substantial detail some of the factors that the agencies will consider in conducting its rule-of-reason analysis of these networks; this discussion of analytical framework is in addition to its separate discussion of integration, joint pricing, and the messenger model (as described previously). These factors can be categorized into five issue areas, which are discussed in greater detail in the following sections: (1) market definition, (2) competitive effects, (3) exclusion of particular providers, (4) efficiencies, and (5) methodology for conducting a review of multiprovider networks.

Market Definition

The product markets for analyzing the competitive effects of multiprovider networks will likely include both the market for networks, if there is a distinct market for networks, and the market for service components of the network that are or could be sold separately outside the network. The relevant geographic market for each relevant product market affected by the multiprovider network will be determined through a factually specific analysis that focuses on the location of reasonable alternatives.

Competitive Effects

The horizontal and vertical competitive effects of an integrated multiprovider network will be evaluated under the rule of reason. Under a horizontal analysis, the agencies will define the relevant markets, consider concentration in those markets, and evaluate the network's overall competitive effects considering all market conditions. Determining concentration in markets affected by the formation of a multiprovider network is one factor, but the conclusion will be based on a more comprehensive analysis. In evaluating competitive effects, the agencies are interested in the ability and willingness of third-party purchasers to switch between different health care providers or networks. The agencies also will examine whether the competing providers in the network are dealing exclusively through the network; exclusive arrangements may raise antitrust concerns.

Under a vertical analysis, a key concern is the extent to which the network's arrangements with its provider members will foreclose competition by impeding the formation and operation of competing networks. Vertical exclusive arrangements that restrict providers in one market from dealing with nonnetwork providers that compete in a different market, or that restrict network members' dealing with insurers, will be examined to determine the degree to which the arrangement limits the ability of other networks or health benefits plans to compete in the relevant markets. In determining if a multiprovider network is nonexclusive, the agencies will rely on the same factors used to evaluate the nonexclusivity of a physician network joint venture.

Exclusion of Particular Providers

The rule of reason will be used in analyzing the exclusion of providers from a multiprovider network. The focus is whether the exclusion reduces competition among providers in the market and harms consumers, not whether a particular provider has been harmed. For example, the exclusion may create competitive concerns if the provider is unable to compete without access to the network or if the exclusion reduces competition among providers. The agencies will also take into account any procompetitive benefits that may justify the exclusion.

Efficiencies

The agencies will balance potential anticompetitive effects of the multiprovider network against the potential efficiencies associated with its formation and operation; the greater the likely anticompetitive effects, the greater must be the likely efficiencies. Efficiencies include cost savings associated with the assumption of financial risk; reduced administrative costs; and improved utilization review, case management, quality assurance, and economies of scale.

In revised language appearing in the *1996 Policy Statements,* the agencies state that they will no longer accept efficiencies claims if the parties are reasonably able to achieve equivalent or comparable savings through means that are significantly less anticompetitive. The agencies explain, however, that they will not mandate a theoretically least restrictive alternative that is not practical in the face of business realities.

Methodology

The agencies have outlined the type of information upon which they will rely in a rule-of-reason analysis, including (but not necessarily limited to) information provided by the members of the multiprovider network, and information gathered through conducting interviews with purchasers, competitors, and the employers who offer the health benefits in question. In conducting these interviews, the agencies will give particular weight to information from purchasers who have tried to switch providers as a result of price increases.

Physician Hospital Organizations

In 1995, the DOJ brought its first two enforcement actions against PHOs in Danbury, Connecticut, and St. Joseph, Missouri, alleging that they illegally conspired to prevent or delay the market entry of managed care plans; both cases were ultimately resolved by consent decree.[280] In both cases, the DOJ alleged that the PHOs exploited their market power illegally to set fees for physician services and thereby thwart efforts by managed care plans to negotiate discounts on physician fees contained in hospital charges. According to the government's complaint, the hospitals in both PHOs were local monopolies, and the majority of physicians in each community were dictating higher prices and other conditions to area managed health care plans. Moreover, the PHOs' physicians were competitors who jointly negotiated fees without engaging in significant financial risk sharing as defined in the agencies' *1994 Policy Statements*.[281]

Under the two consent decrees, which have similar terms, the PHOs in both states agreed to substantially restructure their operations. The decrees prohibited the hospitals and the physicians' groups from owning an interest in any organization that sets fees or other terms of reimbursement for competing physicians unless the organization meets the definition of a "qualified managed care plan" (QMCP). To restructure into a QMCP, the PHO must make changes directed toward tighter integration; for example, where physician contracts are nonexclusive, owners of a QMCP must share substantial financial risk and must comprise no more than 30 percent of the physicians in any relevant market. The decrees also allow the PHOs to retain a basic PHO structure, but only by using a messenger model approach to set physician fees. As defined in the decrees, such an approach requires the use of a third party to negotiate contracts for individual providers, who must make their own separate decisions about a purchaser's proposal, independent of other physicians' decisions and without the messenger's influence.

A year later, the DOJ entered into a similar consent decree with a women's specialty clinic and its affiliated PHO located in Baton Rouge, Louisiana, under which the PHO must restructure into a QMCP.[282] After the DOJ filed suit charging that the hospital and PHO violated antitrust laws by dictating higher prices for physician services and preventing development of competition among area hospitals for inpatient obstetrical services, the defendant-companies entered into negotiations that resulted in an agreement very similar to the decrees issued in the *Danbury* and *St. Joseph* cases: the hospital and PHO must be structured in accordance with the agency's definition of QMCP (i.e., compliance with essentially the same requirements as outlined in the previous consent decrees), and must use a messenger model approach to set physician fees. The consent decree in this case, however, differs from the earlier enforcement actions in that the hospital and PHO must obtain the agency's prior written approval before forming a QMCP.

Additional Agency Guidance

Both the DOJ and the FTC have issued dozens of business review letters and staff advisory opinions commenting on proposals before them. These offer additional guidance in describing situations that practitioners have encountered and on which they seek advice. The usefulness of such information for purposes of predicting agency enforcement initiatives is somewhat limited. Because most requests for such letters involve situations either that fall within the safety zones set forth in the *1996 Policy Statements,* or that do not venture beyond those confines, the agency advice contained in these sources does not address some of the more difficult issues that come before antitrust lawyers on a frequent basis. Nonetheless, health care organizations should consider reviewing relevant agency decisions as a tool for assessing a merger proposal[283] and may want to consider seeking agency advice through the business review or staff advisory process.[284]

NOTES

1. 15 U.S.C. §§ 1 & 2.
2. 15 U.S.C. §§ 13 through 19.
3. 15 U.S.C. § 45.
4. 15 U.S.C. § 13a.
5. Note that price discrimination in violation of antitrust laws is beyond the scope of this book.

6. 15 U.S.C. § 18.

7. Although the majority of states have enacted state antitrust laws, for the most part these laws mirror the federal antitrust statutes, which are the primary focus of this book.

8. 15 U.S.C. § 1.

9. 15 U.S.C. § 2. Note that antitrust law prohibiting monopolization is covered in later sections of this book. Antitrust law prohibiting attempted monopolization, however, is beyond the scope of this book.

10. Section 2 of the Clayton Act originally prohibited price discrimination in sales of commodities, but that section was amended by the Robinson-Patman Act, which now serves that purpose.

11. *See* 15 U.S.C. § 14.

12. *See* 15 U.S.C. § 18 (as amended by the Celler-Kefauver Act).

13. *See* 15 U.S.C. § 15. Note that this remedy is applicable to violations of both the Sherman and Clayton Acts.

14. 15 U.S.C. §§ 41 through 51.

15. 15 U.S.C. § 45.

16. *See, e.g.,* American Medical Ass'n v. United States, 317 U.S. 519 (1943).

17. 421 U.S. 773 (1975).

18. *See, e.g.,* Arizona v. Maricopa County Med. Soc'y, 457 U.S. 332 (1982).

19. Note that antitrust law as it pertains to staff privileges, as well as the substantial amount of case law in this area, is beyond the scope of this book.

20. 15 U.S.C. § 1.

21. 15 U.S.C. §§ 13a & 24.

22. 15 U.S.C. §§ 1311 through 1314.

23. 15 U.S.C. § 16(b) through (h). Increasingly, defendants are using consent decrees as a means to avoid expensive antitrust litigation when the result is fairly certain or when the parties reach agreement on most issues.

24. 15 U.S.C. § 1311.

25. U.S. Department of Justice and the Federal Trade Commission, Clearance Procedures for Investigations (Dec. 2, 1993).

26. 16 C.F.R. §§ 2.1 & 2.2.

27. 16 C.F.R. § 2.7.

28. 15 U.S.C. §§ 45(m) & 53(b).

29. 15 U.S.C. § 15(c).

30. Alabama's antitrust law, for example, imposes on corporations, fines that do not exceed $2,000 (ALA. CODE §§ 8-10-1 through 8-10-3), while New York antitrust law imposes fines on corporations not to exceed $1,000,000 (N.Y. GEN. BUS. LAW §§ 340 through 347).

31. *See, e.g.,* CONN. GEN. STAT. §§ 35-24 through 35-45; FLA. STAT. §§ 542.15 through 542.36.

32. *See* U.S. Department of Justice, the Federal Trade Commission, and the National Association of Attorneys General, Joint Merger Investigation Protocol (Mar. 11, 1998). This document, accessible on the Internet at http://

www.ftc.gov/os/9803/mergerco.op.htm, outlines a general framework for the conduct of joint federal/state merger investigations.

33. Although states' concerns will vary, the National Association of Attorneys General has adopted guidelines that would be applicable to hospital mergers. *See* Horizontal Merger Guidelines of the National Association of Attorneys General, reprinted at 4 Trade Reg. Rep. (CCH) ¶13,406 (1993).

34. 15 U.S.C. § 15.

35. 15 U.S.C. § 26.

36. *See, e.g.,* Illinois Brick v. Illinois, 431 U.S. 720 (1977).

37. *See, e.g.,* Blue Shield v. McCready, 457 U.S. 465 (1982); Huron Valley Hosp., Inc. v. City of Pontiac, 466 F. Supp. 1301 (E.D. Mich. 1979), *rev'd and remanded on other grounds,* 666 F.2d 1029 (6th Cir. 1981).

38. *See, e.g.,* California v. American Stores Co., 495 U.S. 271 (1990).

39. *See, e.g.,* Western Waste Serv. Sys. v. Universal Waste Control & Waste Management Inc., 616 F.2d 1094 (9th Cir.), *cert. denied,* 449 U.S. 869 (1980) (any activity); Seglin v. Esau, 769 F.2d 1274 (7th Cir. 1985) (particular activity).

40. 500 U.S. 322 (1991).

41. *See, e.g.,* Hahn v. Oregon Physicians Serv., 689 F.2d 840 (9th Cir. 1982), *cert. denied,* 462 U.S. 1133 (1983); Shahawy v. Harrison, 778 F.2d 636 (11th Cir. 1985), *opinion amended,* 790 F.2d 75 (11th Cir. 1986).

42. Continental Television, Inc. v. GTE Sylvania, Inc., 433 U.S. 36 (1977).

43. 356 U.S. 1 (1958).

44. Conduct that could be characterized as a group boycott, for example, but which conduct is taken for noncommercial reasons, has been analyzed under the rule of reason.

45. Broadcast Music, Inc. v. Columbia Broadcast Sys., Inc., 441 U.S. 1 (1979).

46. *See, e.g.,* Medical Arts Pharmacy v. Blue Cross & Blue Shield, 518 F. Supp. 1100 (D. Conn. 1981), *aff'd,* 675 F.2d 502 (2d Cir. 1982).

47. 457 U.S. 332 (1982).

48. *See, e.g.,* Wright v. Southern Mono Hosp. Dist., 631 F. Supp. 1294 (E.D. Cal. 1986), *aff'd without opinion,* 924 F.2d 1063 (9th Cir. 1991); McElhinney v. Med. Protective Co., 549 F. Supp. 121 (E.D. Ky. 1982); Pontius v. Children's Hosp., 552 F. Supp. 1352 (W.D. Pa. 1982).

49. 246 U.S. 231 (1918).

50. Federal Trade Comm'n v. Indiana Fed'n of Dentists, 476 U.S. 447 (1986).

51. Federal Trade Comm'n v. Indiana Fed'n of Dentists, 476 U.S. 447 (1986). *See also* Bhan v. NME Hosps., Inc., 669 F. Supp. 998 (E.D. Cal. 1987), *aff'd,* 929 F. 2d 1404 (9th Cir. 1991) (full rule-of-reason analysis not necessary when lesser analysis may show that alleged restraint actually produced reduction in output or other significant anticompetitive effect).

52. *See, e.g.,* Sausalito Pharmacy, Inc. v. Blue Shield, 544 F. Supp. 230 (N.D. Cal. 1981), *aff'd,* 677 F.2d 47 (9th Cir.), *cert. denied,* 459 U.S. 1016 (1982).

53. *See, e.g.,* Kartell v. Blue Shield, 749 F.2d 922 (1st Cir. 1984), *cert. denied,* 471 U.S. 1029 (1985).

54. Monsanto Co. v. Spray-Rite Serv. Corp., 465 U.S. 752 (1984).

55. *See, e.g.,* Nurse Midwifery Assocs. v. Hibbett, 918 F.2d 605 (6th Cir. 1990), *cert. denied sub nom.,* Nurse Midwifery Assocs. v. Hendersonville Community Hosp., 502 U.S. 952 (1991) (conspiracy may be inferred from behavior); Oltz v. St. Peter's Community Hosp., 861 F.2d 1440 (9th Cir. 1988) (direct evidence of conspiracy rare).

56. *See, e.g.,* Oksanen v. Page Mem'l Hosp., 945 F.2d 696 (4th Cir. 1991), *cert. denied,* 502 U.S. 1074 (1992) (mere action of making a peer review recommendation does not prove existence of a conspiracy); Lie v. St. Joseph's Hosp., 964 F.2d 567 (6th Cir. 1992) (granting summary judgment for defendant based on plaintiff's failure to prove market power or otherwise come forward with direct or circumstantial evidence to prove common design to achieve unlawful objective).

57. *See, e.g.,* Hahn v. Oregon Physicians' Serv., 868 F.2d 1022 (9th Cir. 1988), *cert. denied,* 493 U.S. 846 (1989).

58. *See, e.g.,* United States v. E.I. duPont de Nemours & Co., 353 U.S. 586 (1957).

59. *See, e.g.,* United States v. Grinnell Corp., 384 U.S. 563 (1966).

60. *See, e.g.,* Robles v. Humana Hosp. Cartersville, 785 F. Supp. 989 (N.D. Ga. 1992).

61. Based on the majority decision in Jefferson Parish Hosp. Dist. No. 2 v. Hyde, 466 U.S. 2 (1984), it appears that the Supreme Court is likely to favor an approach based on consideration of individual services.

62. *See, e.g.,* Hoffman v. Delta Dental Plan of Minn., 517 F. Supp. 564 (D. Minn. 1981).

63. *See, e.g.,* Robinson v. Magovern, 521 F. Supp. 842 (W.D. Pa. 1981), *aff'd,* 688 F.2d 824 (3d Cir.), *cert. denied,* 459 U.S. 971 (1982).

64. *See, e.g.,* United States v. Hospital Affiliates Int'l, Inc., No. 80-3672 (E.D. La. Oct. 9, 1980) (unpublished).

65. *See* Santa Cruz Med. Clinic v. Dominican Santa Cruz Hosp., No. C93 20613 RWM (N.D. Cal. Sept. 7, 1995) (unpublished).

66. United States v. Long Island Jewish Med. Ctr., 983 F. Supp. 121 (E.D.N.Y. 1997).

67. See Federal Trade Comm'n v. Freeman Hosp., 69 F.3d 260 (8th Cir. 1995).

68. Tampa Elec. Co. v. Nashville Coal Co., 365 U.S. 320 (1961).

69. *See* United States v. Phillipsburg Nat'l Bank, 399 U.S. 350 (1970).

70. Elzinga & Hogarty, *The Problem of Geographic Market Delineation in Antimerger Suits,* 18 ANTITRUST BULL. 45 (1973).

71. 717 F. Supp. 1251 (N.D. Ill. 1989), *aff'd,* 898 F.2d 1278 (7th Cir.), *cert. denied,* 498 U.S. 920 (1990).

72. *See, e.g.,* Morrisey, Sloan & Valvona, *Defining Geographic Markets for Hospital Care,* 51 LAW & CONTEMP. PROBS. 165 (Spring 1988).

73. 69 F.3d 260 (8th Cir. 1995).

74. 521 F. Supp. 842 (W.D. Pa. 1981), *aff'd,* 688 F.2d 824 (3d Cir.), *cert. denied,* 459 U.S. 971 (1982).

75. In more recent cases in the health care realm, courts have found that different types of medical services provided at the same hospital might have different geographic markets. *See, e.g.,* United States v. Carilion Health Sys., 707 F. Supp. 840 (W.D. Va.), *aff'd without op.,* 892 F.2d 1042 (4th Cir. 1989); United States v. Long Island Jewish Med. Ctr., 983 F. Supp. 121 (E.D.N.Y. 1997); Federal Trade Comm'n v. Butterworth Health Corp., 946 F. Supp. 1285 (W.D. Mich. 1996) (unpublished), *aff'd,* No. 96-2440 (6th Cir. July 8, 1997) (unpublished).

76. *See, e.g.,* Sahfi v. St. Francis Hosp., 937 F.2d 603 (4th Cir. 1991) (hospital with 11 percent market share does not have sufficient market power to restrain trade); Jefferson Parish Hosp. Dist. No. 2 v. Hyde, 466 U.S. 2 (1984) (hospital did not have market power when it attracted 30 percent of area residents).

77. *See, e.g.,* Hassan v. Independent Practice Assocs., P.C., 698 F. Supp. 679 (E.D. Mich. 1988) (defendant does not possess market power where its market share is 20 percent in market characterized by other large competitors and no significant barriers to entry); Ball Mem'l Hosp. v. Mutual Hosp. Ins., Inc., 784 F.2d 1325 (7th Cir. 1986), (50 percent market share in relevant market of health care financing did not demonstrate Blue Cross/Blue Shield's market power where market characterized by few barriers to entry and high mobility).

78. *See, e.g.,* United States v. Grinnell Corp., 384 U.S. 563 (1966).

79. *See, e.g.,* Weiss v. York Hosp., 745 F.2d 786 (3d Cir. 1984), *cert. denied,* 470 U.S. 1060 (1985) (monopoly existed with 80 percent market share where only two hospitals in the area provided inpatient services).

80. *See, e.g.,* SmithKline Corp v. Eli Lilly & Co., 575 F.2d 1056 (3d Cir. 1978) (market share between 90 percent to 100 percent constituted monopoly power); Bellavia v. Hackensack Med. Ctr., No. 87-3698 (D.N.J. Sept. 11, 1991) (unpublished) (noting that courts have consistently required showing of at least 70 percent market share to infer market power).

81. 148 F.2d 416 (2d Cir. 1945).

82. *See, e.g.,* Morgenstern v. Wilson, 29 F.3d 1291 (8th Cir. 1994), *cert. denied,* 513 U.S. 1150 (1995) (80 percent market share sufficient but 30 percent insufficient to constitute monopoly power); Blue Cross & Blue Shield United v. Marshfield Clinic, 65 F.3d 1406 (7th Cir. 1995), *cert. denied,* 516 U.S. 1184 (1996) (physician-owned clinic not a monopolist with market share percentage of less than 50 percent).

83. American Bar Association Antitrust Section, Antitrust Law Developments 119-121 (2d ed. 1984).

84. *Compare* Ball Mem'l Hosp., Inc. v. Mutual Hosp. Ins. Inc., 784 F.2d 1325 (7th Cir. 1986) (50 percent market share insufficient to establish market power where few barriers to entry) *with* Reazin v. Blue Cross & Blue Shield of Kan. Inc., 663 F. Supp. 1360 (D. Kan. 1987), *aff'd and remanded,* 899 F.2d 951 (10th Cir.), *cert. denied,* 497 U.S. 1005 (1990) (60 percent market share sufficient to establish monopoly power where no significant barriers to entry existed, but defendant's share was 15 times larger than next largest competitor).

85. *See, e.g.,* Mercy-Peninsula Ambulance, Inc. v. County of San Mateo, 791 F.2d 755 (9th Cir. 1986) ("gravamen of Section 2 claim is the deliberate use of market power"); Potter Med. Ctr. v. City Hosp. Ass'n, 800 F.2d 568 (6th Cir. 1986) (predatory conduct is use of monopoly power to foreclose competition).

86. *See, e.g.,* United States v. Aluminum Co. of Am., 148 F.2d 416 (2d Cir. 1945).

87. United States v. Griffith, 334 U.S. 100 (1948).

88. *See* Key Enters. of Del., Inc. v. Venice Hosp., 919 F.2d 1550 (11th Cir. 1990), *vacated on other grounds,* 979 F.2d 806 (11th Cir. 1992).

89. *See, e.g.,* M & M Med. Supplies & Serv., Inc. v. Pleasant Valley Hosp., Inc., 981 F.2d 160 (4th Cir. 1992), *cert. denied,* 508 U.S. 972 (1993).

90. Advanced Health Care Serv. v. Giles Mem'l Hosp., 846 F. Supp. 488 (W.D. Va. 1994).

91. *See, e.g.,* Otter Tail Power Co. v. United States, 410 U.S. 366 (1973); McKenzie v. Mercy Hosp., 854 F.2d 365 (10th Cir. 1988), *overruled in part, on other grounds;* Systemcore Inc. v. Wang Lab. Corp., 117 F.3d 1137 (10th Cir. 1997).

92. *See, e.g.,* Blue Cross & Blue Shield United v. Marshfield Clinic, 65 F.3d 1406 (7th Cir. 1995), *cert. denied,* 516 U.S. 1184 (1996) (rejecting essential facility claims as applied to physician-owned health care clinic that does not control 50 percent of the market); Tarabishi v. McAlester Reg'l Hosp., 951 F.2d 1558 (10th Cir. 1991), *cert. denied,* 505 U.S. 1206 (1992) (essential facility claim rejected because there was no evidence of hospital's power to control prices).

93. *See, e.g.,* MCI Communications Corp. v. AT&T Co., 708 F.2d 1081 (7th Cir.), *cert. denied,* 464 U.S. 891 (1983).

94. *See, e.g.,* Advanced Health-Care Servs., Inc. v. Radford Community Hosp., 910 F.2d 139 (4th Cir. 1990) (issue for jury of whether access to patients was an essential facility to entry into the DME market); American Health Sys. v. Visiting Nurse Ass'n, 1994-1 Trade Cas. (CCH) ¶70,633 (E.D. Pa. 1994) (if meeting elements of essential facilities claim, hospital may be essential facility as to home health care agencies that rely on hospital's patient referrals). *See also* Advanced Health Care Servs., Inc. v. Giles Mem'l Hosp., 864 F. Supp. 488 (W.D. Va. 1994).

95. *See, e.g.,* Blue Cross & Blue Shield United v. Marshfield Clinic, 65 F.3d 1406 (7th Cir. 1995), *cert. denied,* 516 U.S. 1184 (1996).

96. *See* Advanced Health Care Servs. v. Giles Mem'l Hosp., 846 F. Supp. 488 (W.D. Va. 1994), citing Twin Labs., Inc. v. Weider Health & Fitness, 900 F.2d 566 (2d Cir. 1990).

97. *See, e.g.,* Kartell v. Blue Shield, 749 F.2d 922 (1st Cir. 1984), *cert. denied,* 471 U.S. 1029 (1985) (at minimum, predatory pricing requires that price be below marginal cost).

98. *See, e.g.,* Ocean State Physicians Health Plan, Inc. v. Blue Cross & Blue Shield, 883 F.2d 1101 (1st Cir. 1989), *cert. denied,* 494 U.S. 1027 (1990); Westchester Radiological Assocs., P.C. v. Empire Blue Cross & Blue Shield, Inc.,

707 F. Supp. 708 (S.D.N.Y.), *aff'd per curiam,* 884 F.2d 707 (2d Cir. 1989), *cert. denied,* 493 U.S. 1095 (1990); Kartell v. Blue Shield of Mass., Inc., 749 F.2d 922 (1st Cir. 1984), *cert. denied,* 471 U.S. 1029 (1985).

99. Silver v. New York Stock Exch., 373 U.S. 341 (1963).

100. The NHPRDA was repealed in 1986. *See* National Health Planning and Resources Development Act of 1974, Pub. L. 93-641, 88 Stat. 2226, codified at 42 U.S.C. § 300k through 300n, repealed by Pub. L. 99-660, Title VII, 701(a), 100 Stat. 3799.

101. *See, e.g.,* National Gerimedical Hosp. & Gerontology Ctr. v. Blue Cross, 452 U.S. 378 (1981) (setting forth conditions necessary for implied repeal exemption).

102. *See* Boulware v. State, 960 F.2d 793 (9th Cir. 1992).

103. *See* White & White, Inc. v. American Hosp. Supply Corp., 540 F. Supp. 951 (W.D. Mich. 1982), *rev'd on other grounds,* 723 F.2d 495 (6th Cir. 1983). *See also* Ballard v. Blue Shield, 529 F. Supp. 71 (S.D.W. Va. 1981) (no implied repeal where complaint alleged a group boycott to refuse health insurance coverage for chiropractic services).

104. *Cf.* Jefferson County Pharmaceutical Ass'n v. Abbott Labs., 460 U.S. 150 (1983) (holding that sale of pharmaceutical supplies to state hospitals for resale to consumers was not exempt sale to government under Robinson-Patman Act). *But see* Pharmaceutical & Diagnostic Servs., Inc. v. University of Utah, 801 F. Supp. 508 (D. Utah 1990) (holding university to be state agent and therefore immune from antitrust liability in relation to its operation of radiopharmacy that competed with private enterprises.)

105. *See, e.g.,* Federal Trade Comm'n v. Hospital Bd. of Lee County, 38 F.3d 1184 (11th Cir. 1994) (county hospital board); Todorov v. DCH Healthcare Auth., 891 F.2d 810 (11th Cir. 1991) (state hospital); Bloom v. Hennepin County, 783 F. Supp. 418 (D. Minn. 1992) (county hospital). *But see* Stacy v. Truman Med. Ctr., No. WD 43048 (Mo. Ct. App. Sept. 3, 1991) (unpublished) (doctrine does not apply to city hospital restructured as nonprofit hospital).

106. *See, e.g.,* Federal Trade Comm'n v. University Health, Inc., 938 F.2d 1206 (11th Cir. 1991); Lancaster Community Hosp. v. Antelope Valley Hosp. Dist., 940 F.2d 397 (9th Cir. 1991), *cert. denied,* 502 U.S. 1094 (1992).

107. 471 U.S. 34 (1985).

108. 471 U.S. 48 (1985).

109. 504 U.S. 621 (1992).

110. Martin v. Memorial Hosp., 86 F.3d 1391 (5th Cir. 1996).

111. *See* Askew v. DCH Reg'l Health Care Auth., 995 F.2d 1033 (11th Cir.), *cert. denied,* 510 U.S. 1012 (1993).

112. *See* Federal Trade Comm'n v. Hospital Bd. of Lee County, 38 F.3d 1184 (11th Cir. 1994).

113. *See also* General Hosps. of Humana v. Baptist Med. Sys., No. LR-C-84-455 (E.D. Ark. Feb. 12, 1986) (unpublished). *But see* North Carolina ex rel Edmisten v. P.I.A. Asheville, Inc., 740 F.2d 274 (4th Cir. 1984), *cert. denied,* 471 U.S. 1003 (1985) (state action doctrine does not provide immunity for public

hospital's acquisition, even though hospital had obtained a CON, because state does not "actively supervise" by monitoring hospitals' post-acquisition conduct to ensure that goals of CON program are being satisfied).

114. *See, e.g.,* Patrick v. Burget, 486 U.S. 94 (1988); Summit Health, Ltd. v. Pinhas, 500 U.S. 322 (1991).

115. 486 U.S. 94 (1988).

116. *See* Miller v. Indiana Hosp., 930 F.2d 334 (3d Cir. 1991).

117. *See, e.g.,* Shahawy v. Harrison, 875 F.2d 1529 (11th Cir. 1989); Jiricko v. Coffeyville Mem'l Hosp. Med. Ctr., 700 F. Supp. 1559 (D. Kan. 1988). *But see* Marrese v. Interrequal, Inc., 748 F.2d 373 (7th Cir. 1984).

118. *See* Crosby v. Hospital Auth., 873 F. Supp. 1568 (M.D. Ga. 1995), *aff'd,* 93 F. 3d 1515 (11th Cir. 1996).

119. *See, e.g.,* COLO. REV. STAT. §§ 24-32-2701 through 24-32-2715; FLA. STAT. ch. 395.606; GA. CODE ANN. § 31-7-72.1; KAN. CODE §§ 65-425 & 65-4909; MINN. STAT. ANN. §§ 62J.2911 through 62J.2921; MONT. CODE § 50-4-603(2).

120. *See* Memorial Mission Hosp./St. Joseph's Hosp. (certificate of public advantage issued pursuant to Hospital Cooperation Act of 1993, 1993 N.C. Sess. Laws C. 529).

121. *See* Deaconess Med. Ctr./Columbus Hosp. (certificate of public advantage issued pursuant to MONT. CODE ANN. § 50-4-601).

122. For a general discussion of "certificate of public advantage" processes and their antitrust ramifications, *see* Sarah S. Vance, *Immunity of State-Sanctioned Provider Collaboration After Ticor,* 62 ANTITRUST L.J. 409 (1994).

123. *See, e.g.,* Partners Healthcare System/North Shore Med. Ctr., No. 96-1713B (S. Ct. Mass. 1996); State of Wisconsin v. Kenosha Hosp. & Med. Ctr., 1997-1 Trade Cas. (CCH) ¶71,669 (E.D. Wis. 1996); Southcoast Health System, No. 96-13190F (S. Ct. Mass. 1996); Maine v. Central & W. Me. Reg'l PHO, Inc., 1996-1 Trade Cas. (CCH) ¶17,320 (Me. Super. Ct. 1996); Pennsylvania v. Capital Health Sys. Servs., 1995-2 Trade Cas. (CCH) ¶71,205 (M.D. Pa. 1995); Minnesota v. Children's Health of Saint Paul, No. 4-94-CV-513 (D. Minn. 1995) (unpublished).

124. *See* Maine v. Central & W. Me. Reg'l PHO, Inc. 1996-1 Trade Cas. (CCH) ¶17,320 (Me. Super. Ct. 1996).

125. 15 U.S.C. §§ 34 through 36.

126. *See* Hatch v. North Colo. Med. Ctr., Inc., No. 85-F-2148 (D. Colo. Mar. 27, 1986) (unpublished). *See also* Cohn v. Wilkes Gen. Hosp., 953 F.2d 154 (4th Cir. 1991), *cert. denied,* 505 U.S. 1230 (1992); Sweeney v. Athens Reg'l Med. Ctr., 709 F. Supp. 1563 (M.D. Ga. 1989).

127. *See* Palm Springs Med. Clinic, Inc. v. Desert Hosp., 628 F. Supp. 454 (C.D. Cal. 1986).

128. *See* Sandcrest Outpatient Servs. v. Cumberland County Hosp. Sys., Inc., 853 F.2d 1139 (4th Cir. 1988).

129. *See* Griffith v. Health Care Auth., 705 F. Supp. 1489 (N.D. Ala. 1989).

130. *See* Gold Cross Ambulance v. Kansas City, 705 F.2d 1005 (8th Cir.), *cert. denied,* 471 U.S. 1003 (1985). *See also* Action Ambulance Serv., Inc. v. Atlanticare Health Servs, Inc., 815 F. Supp. 33 (D. Mass. 1993).

131. *See, e.g.,* Huron Valley Hosp., Inc. v. City of Pontiac, 650 F. Supp. 1325 (E.D. Mich. 1986), *aff'd,* 849 F.2d 262 (6th Cir. 1988), *cert. denied,* 488 U.S. 942 (1989).

132. *See, e.g.,* Otter Tail Power Co. v. United States, 410 U.S. 366 (1973); California Motor Transp. v. Trucking Unlimited, 404 U.S. 508 (1972).

133. *See, e.g.,* Surgidev Corp. v. Eye Tech., Inc., 625 F. Supp. 800 (D. Minn. 1986); St. Joseph's Hosp. v. Hospital Corp. of Am., 795 F.2d 948 (11th Cir. 1986) (misrepresentation in CON proceedings); Hospital Building Co. v. Trustees of Rex Hosp., 691 F.2d 678 (1982), *cert. denied,* 464 U.S. 890 (1983) (misrepresentation in CON proceedings).

134. *See* United States v. North Dakota Hosp. Ass'n, 640 F. Supp. 1028 (D.N.D. 1986).

135. *See* Community Blood Bank of Kansas City Area, Inc. v. Federal Trade Comm'n, 405 F.2d 1011 (8th Cir. 1969).

136. *See* Federal Trade Comm'n v. National Comm'n on Egg Nutrition, 517 F.2d 485 (7th Cir. 1975), *cert. denied,* 426 U.S. 919 (1976).

137. 638 F.2d 443 (2d Cir. 1980), *aff'd by an equally divided Court,* 455 U.S. 676 (1982).

138. 15 U.S.C. § 13(c).

139. The Robinson-Patman Act, 15 U.S.C. § 13a, which is not covered in this book, makes it unlawful to discriminate in price between different purchasers of like commodities if the effect of such discrimination may substantially lessen competition.

140. 425 U.S. 1 (1976).

141. 460 U.S. 150 (1983).

142. 743 F.2d 1388 (9th Cir. 1984), *cert. denied,* 469 U.S. 1229 (1985).

143. 21 U.S.C. §§ 301, 331, 333, 353, & 381.

144. *See, e.g.,* Federal Trade Comm'n v. University Health, Inc., 938 F.2d 1206 (11th Cir. 1991). *See also* Adventist Health Sys./W., FTC Dkt. No. 9234 (Aug. 2, 1991).

145. 15 U.S.C. §§ 1011 through 1015.

146. 440 U.S. 205 (1978).

147. *See, e.g.,* Union Labor Life Ins. Co. v. Pireno, 458 U.S. 119 (1982) (exemption does not apply to insurance company's "peer review" process objecting to physician's fees and practices); Ratino v. Medical Serv., 718 F.2d 1269 (4th Cir. 1983) (exemption does not apply to Blue Cross/Blue Shield's "usual, customary and reasonable" standards in provider agreements); Hahn v. Oregon Physicians Serv., 689 F.2d 840 (9th Cir. 1982), *cert. denied,* 462 U.S. 1133 (1983) (exemption does not apply to exclusion of podiatry services from health plan coverage).

148. 899 F.2d 951 (10th Cir.), *cert. denied,* 497 U.S. 1005 (1990). *See also* Hahn v. Oregon Physicians Serv., 689 F.2d 840 (9th Cir. 1982), *cert. denied,* 462 U.S. 1133 (1983) (cautioning that McCarran-Ferguson should not be broadened to exempt insurance companies simply because they have diversified into areas that are not traditionally considered to be business of insurance, such as prepaid health care provider plans).

149. 42 U.S.C. §§ 11101 through 11152.

150. *See* Austin v. McNamara, 979 F.2d 728 (9th Cir. 1992).

151. *See, e.g.,* Smith v. Ricks, 31 F.3d 1478 (9th Cir. 1994), *cert. denied,* 514 U.S. 1035 (1995); Imperial v. Suburban Hosp. Ass'n, 37 F.3d 1026 (4th Cir. 1994); Mathews v. Lancaster Gen. Hosp., 883 F. Supp. 1016 (E.D. Pa. 1995), *aff'd,* 87 F.3d 624 (3d Cir. 1996); Monroe v. AMI Hosps. of Tex., Inc., 877 F. Supp. 1022 (S.D. Tex. 1994); Benjamin v. Aroostook Med. Ctr., 937 F. Supp. 957 (D. Me. 1996), *aff'd,* 113 F.3d 1 (1st Cir.), *cert. denied,* 118 S. Ct. 602 (1997); Egan v. Athol Mem'l Hosp., 971 F. Supp. 37 (D. Mass. 1997), *aff'd,* 1998-1 Trade Cas. (CCH) ¶72,032 (1st Cir. 1998).

152. *See* Bryan v. James E. Holmes Reg'l Med. Ctr., 33 F.3d 1318 (11th Cir. 1994), *cert. denied,* 514 U.S. 1019 (1995).

153. *See* Nicholas v. North Colorado Med. Ctr., No. 93CA1379 (Colo. Ct. App. Feb. 2, 1995) (unpublished).

154. *See, e.g.,* Decker v. IHC Hosp., Inc., 982 F.2d 433 (10th Cir. 1992), *cert. denied,* 509 U.S. 924 (1993); Manion v. Evans, 986 F.2d 1036 (6th Cir.), *cert. denied,* 510 U.S. 818 (1993). *See also* Fobbs v. Holy Cross Health Sys. Corp., 789 F. Supp. 1054 (E.D. Cal. 1992), *aff'd,* 29 F.3d 1439 (9th Cir. 1994), *cert. denied,* 513 U.S. 1127 (1995).

155. United States v. Socony-Vacuum Oil Co., 310 U.S. 150 (1940). *See also* Catalano, Inc. v. Target Sales, Inc., 446 U.S. 643 (1980); United States v. Container Corp. of Am., 393 U.S. 333 (1969).

156. Note that collusive activity that merely *creates pressure to* increase prices has been held to be a per se violation of antitrust law by at least one state court. *See, e.g.,* Minnesota v. Mid-West Minnesota Associated Physicians (Douglas County Dist. Ct. July 2, 1991) (unpublished).

157. 310 U.S. 150 (1940).

158. American Med. Ass'n v. Federal Trade Comm'n, 638 F.2d 443 (2d Cir. 1980), *aff'd by an equally divided Court,* 455 U.S. 676 (1982).

159. *See also* California Dental Ass'n v. Federal Trade Comm'n, 128 F.3d 720 (9th Cir. 1997) (holding state dental association's restrictions on member-dentists' advertisements concerning price and quality of care to be unlawful restraint on competition).

160. 457 U.S. 332 (1982).

161. *See, e.g.,* Glen Eden Hosp., Inc. v. Blue Cross & Blue Shield, Inc., 740 F.2d 423 (8th Cir. 1984); Ratino v. Medical Serv. of the District of Columbia, 718 F.2d 1260 (1983). *But see* Hassan v. Independent Practice Assocs., 698 F. Supp. 679 (E.D. Mich. 1988).

162. *See, e.g.,* Group Life & Health Ins. v. Royal Drug Co., 440 U.S. 205 (1979); Kartell v. Blue Shield, 749 F.2d 922 (1st Cir. 1984), *cert. denied,* 471 U.S. 1029 (1985).

163. *See* United States v. Alston, 974 F.2d 1206 (9th Cir. 1992). *See also* United States v. Lake Country Optometric Soc'y, Crim. No. W-95-CR-114 (W.D. Tex. Dec. 15, 1995) (unpublished) (criminal charges against trade association of optometrists).

164. *See* United States v. Burgstiner, No. CV491-44 (S.D. Ga. April 29, 1991) (unpublished).

165. *See* Arizona v. Maricopa County Med. Soc'y, 457 U.S. 332 (1982). The development of a relative value scale was prohibited as a prophylactic measure by the district court's order in *Maricopa,* although the Supreme Court was silent on whether the development of the scale itself was unlawful.

166. 473 F. Supp. 147 (S.D.N.Y. 1979). Although this decision predates *Maricopa,* it continues to be valid legal precedent.

167. *See* In re Cal. Med. Ass'n, 93 F.T.C. 519 (1979); In re Minn. State Med. Ass'n, 90 F.T.C. 337 (1977); In re Am. College of Radiology, 89 F.T.C. 144 (1977); In re Am. College of Orthopedic Surgeons, 88 F.T.C. 968 (1976); In re Am. College of Obstetricians & Gynecologists, 88 F.T.C. 955 (1976).

168. United States v. Illinois Podiatry Soc'y, Inc., No. 77-C-501 (N.D. Ill. Dec. 6, 1977) (unpublished).

169. In re American Soc'y of Internal Med., 105 F.T.C. 505 (1985).

170. 446 U.S. 643 (1980).

171. 737 F.2d 1433 (5th Cir. 1984), *cert. denied,* 469 U.S. 1160 (1985).

172. This form of compensation, however, is becoming less frequent as plans are increasingly negotiating contracts that include a plan-designated fee schedule, or that provide for some other form of compensation (i.e., capitation).

173. 472 U.S. 284 (1985).

174. *See* White & White, Inc. v. American Hosp. Supply Corp., 723 F.2d 495 (6th Cir. 1983). *See also* Ohio Hospital Purchasing Consortium, DOJ Business Review Letter (June 9, 1982). (DOJ declined to challenge a proposed group purchasing program that sought to combine eight purchasing groups representing a majority of the nonprofit hospitals in Ohio for purposes of obtaining volume discounts on X-ray film, furniture, and other items.)

175. *See* Langston Corp. v. Standard Register Co., 553 F. Supp. 632 (N.D. Ga. 1982).

176. *See* 23 R.I. Gen. Laws § 23-17-28.

177. *See, e.g.,* Mandeville Island Farms, Inc. v. American Crystal Sugar Co., 334 U.S. 219 (1948); National Macaroni Manufacturers Ass'n v. Federal Trade Comm'n, 345 F.2d 421 (7th Cir. 1965).

178. For a general discussion of hospital group purchasing and the hospital supply market, see Andrew K. Dolan, *What Are the Antitrust Implications of Shared Purchasing for Hospitals,* Hospitals, Oct. 16, 1979, at 76. The article explains that, although hospitals may be the dominant buyers in some markets (e.g., injectable pharmaceuticals, medical supplies, certain medical equipment such as CT scanners), market dominance is highly unlikely because the geographic markets for these products are very large and may even be nationwide in scope. With respect to hospital group purchasing arrangements involving the purchase of nonmedical items (e.g., food, linen, lightbulbs, customized forms) for which the geographic markets are small and local in scope, buyers' market power is unlikely because there are many

competing buyers, including large commercial industries (e.g., restaurants and hotels).

179. U.S. DEPARTMENT OF JUSTICE AND THE FEDERAL TRADE COMMISSION, STATEMENTS OF ANTITRUST ENFORCEMENT POLICY IN HEALTH CARE (Aug. 28, 1996).

180. 737 F.2d 1433 (5th Cir. 1984), *cert. denied,* 469 U.S. 1160 (1985).

181. Sausalito Pharmacy, Inc. v. Blue Shield, 677 F.2d 47 (9th Cir.), *cert. denied,* 459 U.S. 1016 (1982).

182. *See also* Feldman v. Health Care Servs. Corp., 562 F. Supp. 941 (N.D. Ill. 1982); Medical Arts Pharmacy of Stamford, Inc. v. Blue Cross & Blue Shield, Inc., 518 F. Supp. 1100 (D. Conn. 1981); Blue Cross & Blue Shield v. Michigan Ass'n of Psychotherapy Clinics, No. 9-71014 (E.D. Mich. Mar. 14, 1980) (unpublished).

183. Brillhart v. Mutual Med. Ins., 768 F.2d 196 (7th Cir. 1985).

184. Barry v. Blue Cross, 805 F.2d 866 (9th Cir. 1986). *See also* Zinser v. Rose, 868 F.2d 938 (7th Cir. 1989) (nothing unlawful about arrangement whereby insurance companies set limits on amounts insureds may be reimbursed).

185. 422 F.2d 546 (7th Cir. 1970).

186. No. 9-71014 (E.D. Mich. Mar. 14, 1980) (unpublished).

187. Ocean State Physicians Health Plan, Inc. v. Blue Cross, 883 F.2d 1101 (1st Cir. 1989), *cert. denied,* 494 U.S. 1027 (1990).

188. Blue Cross & Blue Shield United v. Marshfield Clinic, 65 F.3d 1406 (7th Cir. 1995) (amended opinion), *cert. denied,* 516 U.S. 1184 (1996).

189. Civil No. 94-1793 PHXPGR (D. Ariz. May 19, 1995), reported at 1995-1 Trade Cas. (CCH) ¶71,048 (D. Ariz. 1995).

190. *See, e.g.,* United States v. Vision Serv. Plan, No. 94-2693 (D.D.C. Jan. 26, 1995) (unpublished); United States v. Oregon Dental Serv., 1995-2 Trade Cas. (CCH) ¶71,602 (N.D. Cal. 1995); RxCare of Tenn., Inc., No. 951-0059 (F.T.C. June 10, 1996) (complaint and final order); United States v. Delta Dental, 943 F. Supp. 172 (D.R.I. 1996).

191. *See, e.g.,* Commonwealth v. Providence Health Sys. 1994-1 Trade Cas. (CCH) ¶70,603 (M.D. Pa. 1994) (consent decree); Commonwealth v. Capital Health Sys. Serv., 1995-2 Trade Cas. (CCH) ¶71,205 (M.D. Pa. 1995) (consent decree).

192. *See* United States v. Delta Dental, 943 F. Supp. 172 (D.R.I. 1996).

193. Kartell v. Blue Shield, 749 F.2d 922 (1st Cir. 1984), *cert. denied,* 471 U.S. 1029 (1985).

194. *See* Westchester Radiological Assocs. v. Empire Blue Cross & Blue Shield, Inc., 884 F.2d 707 (2d Cir. 1989), *cert. denied,* 493 U.S. 1095 (1990).

195. *See* United States v. Topco Assocs., Inc., 405 U.S. 596 (1972). *See also* Palmer v. BRG of Ga., Inc., 498 U.S. 46 (1990).

196. *See, e.g.,* Blue Cross & Blue Shield United v. Marshfield Clinic, 65 F.3d 1406 (7th Cir.), *cert. denied,* 516 U.S. 1184 (1996).

197. *See* State v. Aloupis, 1993-1 Trade Cas. (CCH) ¶70,152 (Me. Super. Ct. 1993).

198. *See also* Anesthesia Advantage, Inc. v. Metz Group, 759 F. Supp. 638 (D. Colo. 1991) (market allocation claims based on hospital call schedule agreed upon in contract between hospital and independent anesthesiologist group).

199. 438 U.S. 531 (1978).

200. 472 U.S. 284 (1985).

201. U.S. Health Care, Inc. v. Healthsource, Inc., 986 F.2d 589 (1st Cir. 1993).

202. 663 F. Supp. 1360 (D. Kan. 1987), *aff'd,* 899 F.2d 951 (10th Cir.), *cert. denied,* 497 U.S. 1005 (1990).

203. *See* Northwest Med. Labs., Inc. v. Blue Cross & Blue Shield, Inc., 794 P.2d 428 (Or. 1990).

204. *See* Capital Imaging Assocs. v. Mohawk Valley Med. Assocs., Inc., 791 F. Supp. 956 (N.D.N.Y. 1992), *aff'd,* 996 F.2d 537 (2d Cir.), *cert. denied,* 510 U.S. 947 (1993). *See also* Betkerur v. Aultman Hosp. Ass'n, 78 F.3d 1079 (6th Cir. 1996).

205. *See* Hassan v. Independent Practice Assocs., 698 F. Supp. 679 (E.D. Mich. 1988).

206. Although not covered in this book, there is a substantial amount of case law in the area of antitrust and denial of staff privileges.

207. 476 U.S. 447 (1986).

208. *See* In re Med. Staff of Good Samaritan Med. Ctr., F.T.C. Dkt. No. C-3554, reported at 60 Fed. Reg. 10,864 (1995).

209. *See also* In re Med. Staff of Broward Gen. Med. Ctr., F.T.C. Dkt. No. C-3344, reprinted at 56 Fed. Reg. 49,185 (1991); In re Med. Staff of Holy Cross Hosp., F.T.C. Dkt. No. C-3345, reprinted at 56 Fed. Reg. 49,184 (1991); In re Med. Staff of Doctors' Hosp. of Prince George's County, 110 F.T.C. 476 (1988).

210. *See* Jefferson Parish Hosp. Dist. No. 2 v. Hyde, 466 U.S. 2 (1984).

211. 448 F.2d 43 (9th Cir. 1971), *cert. denied,* 405 U.S. 955 (1972).

212. Northern Pac. Ry. Co. v. United States, 356 U.S. 1 (1958).

213. *See* Fortner Enters., Inc. v. United States Steel Corp., 394 U.S. 495 (1969).

214. *See, e.g.,* Action Ambulance Serv. v. Atlanticare Health Servs., 815 F. Supp. 33 (D. Mass. 1993).

215. 466 U.S. 2 (1984).

216. *See, e.g.,* Tampa Elec. Co. v. Nashville Coal Co., 365 U.S. 320 (1961). In most cases, exclusive agreements are analyzed under the Clayton Act. Cases involving services, however, must be analyzed under the Sherman Act, as they are beyond the scope of the Clayton Act. The analysis is largely the same, however.

217. *See, e.g.,* Federal Trade Comm'n v. Motion Picture Adver. Serv. Co., 344 U.S. 392 (1953).

218. *See, e.g.,* Twin City Sportservice, Inc. v. Charles O. Finley & Co., 676 F.2d 1291 (9th Cir.), *cert. denied,* 459 U.S. 1009 (1982), in which a 10-year exclusive dealing contract that foreclosed 24 percent of market was held to be illegal.

219. *See, e.g.,* Continental Television, Inc. v. GTE Sylvania, Inc., 433 U.S. 36 (1977).
220. *See, e.g.,* Jefferson Parish Hosp. Dist. No. 2 v. Hyde, 466 U.S. 2 (1984) (30 percent market share insufficient to demonstrate unreasonable restraint of trade).
221. *See* Anesthesia Care, Ltd. v. Passavant Mem'l Hosps. Ass'n, 36 F.3d 664 (7th Cir. 1994). *See also* Balaklaw v. Lovell, 14 F.3d 793 (2d Cir. 1994); U.S. Healthcare, Inc. v. Healthsource, Inc., 1992-1 Trade Cas. (CCH) ¶69,697 (D. N.H. 1992), *aff'd,* 986 F.2d 589 (1st Cir. 1993); Smith v. Northern Mich. Hosps., Inc., 703 F.2d 942 (6th Cir. 1983).
222. *See, e.g.,* Smith v. Northern Mich. Hosps., Inc., 703 F.2d 942 (6th Cir. 1983); Bellam v. Clayton County Hosp. Auth., 758 F.Supp. 1488 (N.D. Ga. 1990). *See also* U.S. Healthcare, Inc. v Healthsource, Inc., 986 F.2nd 589 (1st Cir. 1993) (exclusive contract between physicians and HMO).
223. Federal Trade Comm'n v. Indiana Fed'n of Dentists, 476 U.S. 447 (1986).
224. *See, e.g.,* Virginia Excelsior Mills, Inc. v. Federal Trade Comm'n, 256 F.2d 538 (4th Cir. 1958).
225. F.T.C. Dkt. No. 9129 (Feb. 17, 1983) (unpublished).
226. United States v. North Shore Univ. Hosp. (E.D.N.Y. Dec. 5, 1994) (unpublished consent decree).
227. 438 U.S. 422 (1978).
228. United States v. Utah Soc'y for Healthcare Human Resources Admin., No. 94C282G (D. Utah. Sept. 14, 1994) (unpublished).
229. U.S. DEPARTMENT OF JUSTICE AND THE FEDERAL TRADE COMMISSION, STATEMENTS OF ANTITRUST ENFORCEMENT POLICY IN THE HEALTH CARE AREA (Aug. 28, 1996), at Statements 4, 5, and 6.
230. *See* Murphy, *Application of Federal Antitrust Laws to Hospital Mergers: Understanding the Evolving Rules,* 23 J. HEALTH & HOSP. L. 101 (1990).
231. The DOJ and the FTC jointly issued Horizontal Merger Guidelines in 1992. *See* 1992 Horizontal Merger Guidelines, reported at 57 Fed. Reg. 41,552 (1992) (hereinafter 1992 Merger Guidelines).
232. *See* United States v. Philadelphia Nat'l Bank, 374 U.S. 321 (1963).
233. *See* United States v. Continental Can Co., 378 U.S. 441 (1964).
234. *See* United States v. Von's Grocery Co., 384 U.S. 270 (1966).
235. 1992 Merger Guidelines, 57 Fed. Reg. 41,552 (1992).
236. *See, e.g.,* Philip Proger & Stephen Kiess, *New Developments with Respect to Provider Mergers,* in ANTITRUST DEVELOPMENTS FOR HEALTH CARE PROVIDERS, MONOGRAPH NO. 2 (Forum on Health Law of the American Bar Association, Mar. 1995).
237. 106 F.T.C. 361 (1985).
238. Healthtrust, Inc.—The Hospital Co., F.T.C. File No. 941-0020 (July 11, 1994). *See also* AMERICAN HOSPITAL ASSOCIATION, THE 1994 AHA GUIDE (1994).
239. *See, e.g.,* United States v. Hospital Affiliates Int'l, Inc., No. 80-3672 (E.D. La. 1982) (unpublished consent decree enjoining merger of two psychiatric

hospitals); American Med. Int'l, Inc., 104 F.T.C. 1 (1984) (ordering divesture of hospital); Columbia Hosp. Corp., No. 93-30-CIV-FTM-23D (M.D. Fla. May 5, 1993) (preliminary injunction of hospital corporation's acquisition of hospital, which led to consent decree under which corporation agreed to abandon transaction).

240. 69 F.3d 260 (8th Cir. 1995).

241. 902 F. Supp. 968 (N.D. Iowa 1995). Note that this case was later vacated as moot because the merger was eventually abandoned.

242. U.S. Department of Justice and the Federal Trade Commission, Statements of Antitrust Enforcement Policy in Health Care (Aug. 28, 1996). Note that these policy statements supersede earlier version of the statements issued in 1993 and 1994, but Statement 1 has remained the same in all three versions.

243. 1992 Merger Guidelines, 57 Fed. Reg. 41,552 (1992), at § 0.2.

244. *See* Commonwealth of Pa. v. Providence Health Sys., Inc., 1994-1 Trade Cas. (CCH) ¶70,603 (M.D. Pa. 1994).

245. *See* United States v. Morton Plant Health Sys., Inc. and Trustees of Mease Hospital, Inc. No. 94-748-CIV-T-23E (M.D. Fla. Sept. 29, 1994), reported at 1994-2 Trade Cas. (CCH) ¶70, 759.

246. 898 F.2d 1278 (7th Cir. 1990), *aff'g,* 717 F. Supp. 1251 (N.D. Ill. 1989), *cert. denied,* 498 U.S. 920 (1990).

247. *See also* Federal Trade Comm'n v. University Health, Inc., 938 F.2d 1206 (11th Cir. 1991).

248. 892 F.2d 1042 (4th Cir. 1989), *aff'g,* 707 F. Supp. 840 (W.D. Va. 1989).

249. *Cf.* Federal Trade Comm'n v. University Health, Inc., 938 F.2d 1206 (11th Cir. 1991) (holding that nonprofit status does not prevent hospitals from engaging in anticompetitive behavior).

250. 946 F. Supp. 1285 (W.D. Mich. 1996) (unpublished), *aff'd,* No. 96-2440 (6th Cir. July 8, 1997) (unpublished). *See also* United States v. Long Island Jewish Med. Ctr., 983 F. Supp. 121 (E.D.N.Y. 1997).

251. Cargill, Inc. v. Monfort of Colo., Inc., 479 U.S. 104 (1986).

252. *See, e.g.,* United States Steel Corp. v. Federal Trade Comm'n, 426 F.2d 592 (6th Cir. 1970); United States v. Kennecott Copper Corp., 231 F. Supp. 95 (S.D.N.Y. 1964), *aff'd,* 381 U.S. 414 (1965) (per curiam).

253. In an oligopolistic market, firms engage in parallel pricing and production control to achieve excess profits. A perceived potential competitor has procompetitive effects as it moderates this anticompetitive practice. *See generally* United States v. Black & Decker Mfg. Co., 430 F. Supp. 729 (D. Md. 1976).

254. 1992 Merger Guidelines, 57 Fed. Reg. 41,552 (1992).

255. 15 U.S.C. § 18a.

256. If a health care organization acquires a company engaged in manufacturing, premerger notification is required if the company has total assets or net sales of $10 million or more and the acquiring organization has total assets or annual net sales of $100 million or more, or if the acquired company has total assets or annual net sales of $100 million or more and the acquiring organization has total assets or annual net sales of $10 million or more.

257. *See* 16 C.F.R. Parts 801 & 802.
258. *See* International Shoe Co. v. Federal Trade Comm'n, 280 U.S. 291 (1930).
259. *See* Citizen Publishing Co. v. United States, 394 U.S. 131 (1969); United States v. Reed Roller Bit Co., 274 F. Supp. 573 (W.D. Okla. 1967).
260. 1992 Merger Guidelines, 57 Fed. Reg. 41,552 (1992).
261. 285 N.W.2d 455 (Mich. Ct. App. 1979). *Oleksy* was decided under the Michigan antitrust law, which was patterned after the Sherman Act.
262. It should be noted that in the 1984 Horizontal Merger Guidelines, the DOJ characterized efficiency as a mitigating factor relevant to the Department's determination of whether to initiate legal action rather than as a defense. 49 Fed. Reg. 26,823 (1984). This change in characterization made little difference as a practical matter.
263. *See* United States v. Von's Grocery Co., 384 U.S. 270 (1966).
264. 1992 Merger Guidelines, 57 Fed. Reg. 41,552 (1992).
265. Revision to the Horizontal Merger Guidelines, Section 4: Efficiencies (issued by the U.S. Department of Justice and the Federal Trade Commission, Apr. 8, 1997).
266. Brodley, *The Legal Status of Joint Ventures under the Antitrust Laws: A Summary Assessment,* 21 ANTITRUST BULL. 453 (1976).
267. *Cf.* United States v. Falstaff Brewing Corp., 410 U.S. 526 (1973).
268. *See* Key Enters., v. Venice Hosp., 9 F.3d 893 (11th Cir. 1993), *cert. denied,* 511 U.S. 1126 (1994).
269. *See* Advanced Health-Care Servs. v. Giles Mem'l Hosp., 846 F. Supp. 488 (W.D. Va. 1994).
270. *See* U.S. DEPARTMENT OF JUSTICE AND THE FEDERAL TRADE COMMISSION, STATEMENTS OF ANTITRUST ENFORCEMENT POLICY IN HEALTH CARE (Aug. 28, 1996), at Statement 2.
271. *See* U.S. DEPARTMENT OF JUSTICE AND THE FEDERAL TRADE COMMISSION, STATEMENTS OF ANTITRUST ENFORCEMENT POLICY IN HEALTH CARE (Aug. 28, 1996), at Statement 3.
272. *See* U.S. DEPARTMENT OF JUSTICE AND THE FEDERAL TRADE COMMISSION, STATEMENTS OF ANTITRUST ENFORCEMENT POLICY IN HEALTH CARE (Aug. 28, 1996), at Statement 7.
273. *See* Physician Agreement To Control Medical Prepayment Plans, 46 Fed. Reg. 48,982 (1981).
274. *See, e.g.,* Barry v. Blue Cross, 805 F.2d 866 (9th Cir. 1986).
275. *See* Doctor's Hosp. of Jefferson, Inc. v. Southeast Med. Alliance Inc., 123 F.3d 301 (5th Cir. 1997).
276. *See* EGH, Inc. v. Blue Cross & Blue Shield, No. 90-1210-FR (D. Or. Sept. 26, 1991) (unpublished).
277. 784 F.2d 1325 (7th Cir. 1986).
278. *See, e.g.,* Kartell v. Blue Shield, 749 F.2d 922 (1st Cir. 1984), *cert. denied,* 471 U.S. 1029 (1985).
279. *See* U.S. DEPARTMENT OF JUSTICE AND THE FEDERAL TRADE COMMISSION, ANTITRUST ENFORCEMENT POLICY IN HEALTH CARE (Aug. 28, 1996), at Statements 8 and 9.
280. *See* United States & State of Conn. v. Healthcare Partners, Inc., No. 395-CV-01946-RNC (D. Conn. Sept. 13, 1995); United States v. Health Choice of

Northwest Mo., Inc., No. 95-6171-CV-SJ-6 (W.D. Mo. Sept. 13, 1995) (unpublished consent decrees).

281. Note that this case was litigated before the agencies issued their 1996 *Policy Statements;* thus, under the 1994 *Policy Statements,* joint pricing among physician-members of a PHO was lawful only upon a showing of substantial financial risk sharing.

282. *See* United States v. Woman's Hosp. Found., No. 96-389-B-M2 (M.D. La. Apr. 23, 1996) (unpublished consent decree).

283. FTC staff advisory opinions are available from the Public Reference Branch at (202) 326-2222; they are also available on the Internet at http://www.ftc.gov. Similarly, the DOJ's business review letters are available from the Legal Procedure Unit at (202) 514-2481, as well as from the Internet at http://www.usdoj.gov.

284. *See, e.g.,* 16 C.F.R. § 1.1 (outlining procedure for obtaining, and effect of, FTC staff advisory opinions), and 26 C.F.R. § 50.6 (outlining procedure for obtaining, and effect of, DOJ business review letters).

Index

F

G

H

I

J

9 780834 212275

Printed in Dunstable, United Kingdom

88190714R10090